T0318262

Hermeneutic Moral Realism in Psychology

Traditional sources of morality—philosophical ethics, religious standards, and cultural values—are being questioned at a time when we most need morality's direction. Research shows that moral direction is vital to our identities, happiness, productivity, and relationships, but there is a decline in its development and use, especially among younger adults.

This book argues that hermeneutic moral realism is the best hope for meeting the twenty-first-century challenges of scientism, individualism, and postmodernism. In addition to providing a thorough understanding of moral realism, the volume also takes preliminary steps toward its application in important practical settings, including research, psychotherapy, politics, and publishing.

Brent D. Slife is a clinical psychologist who was, until his recent retirement, Professor of Psychology at Brigham Young University, USA. He is the Editor-in-Chief of the *Journal of Theoretical and Philosophical Psychology* and received the Presidential Citation from the American Psychological Association for his contribution to psychology.

Stephen C. Yanchar is Associate Professor in the Department of Instructional Psychology and Technology at Brigham Young University, USA. He is primarily interested in theoretical and philosophical issues in education and psychology, especially those pertaining to agency and learning, qualitative inquiry, and design practices.

Advances in Theoretical and Philosophical Psychology

Series Editor

Brent D. Slife
Brigham Young University

Brent D. Slife, Kari A. O'Grady, and Russell D. Kosits
The Hidden Worldviews of Psychology's Theory, Research, and Practice

Edwin E. Gantt and Richard N. Williams
On Hijacking Science: Exploring the Nature and Consequences of Overreach in Psychology

Brian Schiff
Situating Qualitative Methods in Psychological Science

Brent D. Slife and Stephen Yanchar
Hermeneutic Moral Realism in Psychology: Theory and Practice

For more information about this series, please visit https://www.routledge.com/psychology/series/TPP

Hermeneutic Moral Realism in Psychology: Theory and Practice

Edited by Brent D. Slife and Stephen C. Yanchar

Routledge
Taylor & Francis Group
New York London

First published 2019
by Routledge
605 Third Avenue, New York, NY 10017

and by Routledge
2 Park Square, Milton Park, Abingdon, Oxon, OX14 4RN

First issued in paperback 2021

Routledge is an imprint of the Taylor & Francis Group, an informa business

Publisher's Note
The publisher has gone to great lengths to ensure the quality of this reprint
but points out that some imperfections in the original copies may be
apparent.

Library of Congress Cataloging-in-Publication Data
A catalog record for this title has been requested

ISBN 13: 978-0-367-56760-6 (pbk)
ISBN 13: 978-1-138-59453-1 (hbk)

Typeset in Times New Roman
by Apex CoVantage LLC

To our sons,
Conor, Nathan, and Jacob
and
Joseph, Jacob, and Alex

Contents

Introduction: Moral Grounds in the Postmodern Era: The Reality of Hermeneutic Morality in Psychology   1

BRENT D. SLIFE AND STEPHEN C. YANCHAR

SECTION 1   19

1   **Hermeneutic Moral Realism, Participational Agency, and World Disclosure**   21

STEPHEN C. YANCHAR AND BRENT D. SLIFE

2   **The Moral Hermeneutic of Scientific Justification**   37

JOSHUA W. CLEGG

3   **Culture and Hermeneutic Moral Realism**   51

JACOB R. HICKMAN

SECTION 2   69

4   **Psychotherapy and the Moral Realism of Charles Taylor**   71

BRENT D. SLIFE, ERIC A. GHELFI, AND NATHAN M. SLIFE

5   **The Moral Affordances of Publishing Practices**   86

JOSHUA W. CLEGG

6   Politics and Moral Realism   97

FRANK C. RICHARDSON, ROBERT C. BISHOP, AND
KATHLEEN L. SLANEY

7   Inquiry Into Moral Configurations   116

STEPHEN C. YANCHAR AND SUSAN PETERSON GONG

   Index   128

Editor and Contributor Biographies

Robert C. Bishop is Associate Professor of Physics and Philosophy and the John and Madeleine McIntyre Professor of History and Philosophy of Science at Wheaton College. His publications include *The Philosophy of the Social Sciences* (Continuum, 2007).

Joshua W. Clegg is Associate Professor of Psychology at John Jay College of Criminal Justice and a member of the faculty in the Critical Social and Personality Psychology doctoral program at The Graduate Center, CUNY.

Eric A. Ghelfi is a clinical psychology Ph.D. student at Brigham Young University. His interests include the philosophy of social science and reproducibility issues in psychology.

Susan Peterson Gong holds a Ph.D. from the Department of Instructional Psychology and Technology at Brigham Young University. She is interested in learning theory with an emphasis on the student practice of asking questions. She is also interested in qualitative inquiry and the philosophical and practical implications of student agency for instructional design.

Jacob R. Hickman is Associate Professor of Anthropology at Brigham Young University. His research spans the fields of cultural psychology, psychological anthropology, religious studies, and Southeast Asian studies.

Frank C. Richardson is Professor of Educational Psychology Emeritus at the University of Texas, Austin. He is author or editor of several books, including *Re-envisioning Psychology* and *Critical Thinking about Psychology*.

Kathleen L. Slaney is Professor of Psychology at Simon Fraser University. She is author of *Validating Psychological Constructs* (2017), and co-editor of *A Wittgensteinian Perspective on the Use of Conceptual Analysis in Psychology* (2013) and *The Wiley Handbook of Theoretical and Philosophical Psychology* (2015).

Brent D. Slife is a clinical psychologist who was, until his recent retirement, Professor of Psychology at Brigham Young University. He is the Editor-in-Chief of the *Journal of Theoretical and Philosophical Psychology* and received the Presidential Citation from the American Psychological Association for his contribution to psychology.

Nathan M. Slife is Assistant Professor-in-Residence in the Department of Educational Psychology and Higher Education at the University of Nevada, Las Vegas. He has been honored with the UNLV College of Education 2016 Distinguished Teaching Award. Dr. Slife is primarily interested in the theoretical foundations and values of higher education and the study of higher education.

Stephen C. Yanchar is Associate Professor in the Department of Instructional Psychology and Technology at Brigham Young University. He is primarily interested in theoretical and philosophical issues in education and psychology, especially those pertaining to agency and learning, qualitative inquiry, and design practices.

Introduction

Moral Grounds in the Postmodern Era: The Reality of Hermeneutic Morality in Psychology

Brent D. Slife and Stephen C. Yanchar

Morality is shaping up to be one of the most significant issues of the twenty-first century. Traditional sources of morality—philosophical ethics, religious standards, and cultural values—are all being questioned at a time when we need morality's direction the most. Indeed, psychologists had not recognized just how pivotal moral direction was until recently. They had long understood morality's importance for value-laden decision making, but recent psychological investigations have demonstrated its significance for our very identities. Research shows, for example, that the eventual loss of identity for Alzheimer patients is more associated with declining moral compass than with failing memory, diminishing personality, or even dwindling happiness (Strohminger & Nichols, 2015). Similar findings reveal that people who have a good moral compass are more grounded, focused, content, and productive (Borgonovi, 2008; Dunn, Aknin, & Norton, 2008; James, 2011). They not only have more nurturing and positive relationships but also give back to the world at least as much as they take (Fowers, 2005).

Regrettably, this research has also documented a decline in the development and use of moral compass. As a telling example, sociologist Christian Smith and his colleagues show with hundreds of detailed interviews how young adults in America (ages 18–23) follow a "hyper-individualist" moral strategy that basically boils down to getting what they want (Smith, Christoffersen, Davidson, & Herzog, 2011). In other words, these investigators found little evidence for any conventional moral direction at all, certainly little moral conscience about the greater good. When these young adults were invited to consider right and wrong, they generally "reflect[ed] weak thinking" (p. 60). "The vast majority of emerging adults could not engage in a discussion about real moral dilemmas," something Smith and his colleagues attributed to "postmodern relativism" (p. 55). Rarely, for instance, did these young adults rely on moral traditions, whether philosophical, religious, or cultural. Instead, their basic "moral" position was that individuals should invent their own rules and do what is best for them.

With this age group one might expect higher education to come to the rescue, teaching better ethics and moral reasoning. Unfortunately, as Barry Schwartz (1987) and Chris Hedges (2009) have argued, higher education appears to be more the problem than the solution. Schwartz, in particular, has detailed how the higher educational system in America just a century ago taught moral philosophy to facilitate common values and shared objectives. However, the growth of science and its stripping of value-laden biases from "objective knowledge" has led higher education to become the location for objectivity, with morality confined to the dustbin of subjectivity. This movement, Schwartz believes, has left young adults with a loss of moral direction: "they don't seem to know where they belong. They don't seem to know that they are doing the right things with their lives. They don't seem to know what the right things are" (p. 4). And Hedges, some 20 years later, heartily agrees. He contends that today's universities have embraced "moral nihilism," where the faculties of these institutions "have forgotten, or never knew, that moral traditions are the products of civilization" (p. 96). In fact, from Hedges perspective, these institutions have become "irrelevant" as a moral force for good.

What's going on? If moral direction is really vital to our identities as well as our contentment, productivity, and relationships, then what has sapped the moral fiber and energy from our nation? As these investigators have collectively discerned, there seems to be a perfect storm of societal and intellectual movements that have led to this predicament. We cannot detail the many societal conditions that have culminated in this storm, but we can point to three of the main culprits facilitated by these conditions and highlighted by Schwartz, Hedges, and Smith: the rise of science (or perhaps scientism), a surge in individualism, and an increased acceptance of postmodernism, especially in university settings.

Each of these movements has undoubtedly advanced many good things, but their collective side effects have facilitated the decline of moral direction. As Schwartz has noted, the reification of a particular view of science (more aptly labeled as "scientism," Gantt & Williams, 2018), has led to the apparent separation of objective and subjective knowledge. Morality, in this view, is relegated to the subjective, more inferior realm of knowing. And as Smith and his colleagues (2011) have observed, individualism and postmodernism have factored significantly in this storm. Both movements have, each in its own unique way, cast doubt on the validity and usefulness of moral traditions, leaving individuals to fend for themselves morally. These three factors, which we will address to some degree in other chapters, have effectively removed any *grounding* for individual decisions about our moral compass.

The present book, however, is less about the problems that have led to this moral situation and more about what we believe is a major part of the solution: hermeneutic moral realism. We will argue that this form of moral grounding is our best hope for standing up to the twenty-first-century challenges of scientism, individualism, and postmodernism. This introductory chapter begins with a brief explanation of moral realism generally. The major portion of this chapter, however, provides a moral illustration in which many of the traditional resources for resolving this illustration are revealed to have significant, twenty-first-century problems. More specifically, we believe that the modern dualism of these traditional resources—their separation into subjective and objective categories—has hampered them irreparably. Although these dualist approaches have frequently been helpful to understand morality, we believe that many are internally inconsistent and others fail to illuminate our fundamental experience of morality. Consequently, we offer a nondualist (hermeneutic) approach to this illustration that will serve to introduce our moral solution. The remainder of the book, then, fleshes out this solution by providing a conceptual understanding as well as particular applications of this understanding to psychotherapy, politics, research, and culture.

Moral Realism

As the phrase "moral realism" would imply, the authors of this book will contend that there is a kind of reality to morality. In other words, human life involves non-arbitrary, non-conventional normative demands that are not only involved in our ethics and values but also give us the reasons for the vast majority of our actions. As Alasdair MacIntyre (1988) put it, "Psychologies express . . . and presuppose moralities" (p. 77). The realist claim is that the moral good is *not* good because some individual happens to like it (individualism) or even because some culture happens to like it (postmodernism). Rather, the realist claim is that we *ought* to like what is morally good. To quote Charles Taylor (1989), "What is real is what you have to deal with, what won't go away just because it doesn't fit with your prejudices" (p. 59). We will argue with regard to moral realism that important aspects of morality simply won't go away, even if they don't fit our prejudices, and these aspects, we will further argue, will allow us to ground morality in our twenty-first-century world.

Given the popularity of individualism within American society (Fowers, Richardson, & Slife, 2017; Triandis, 2018) and postmodernism within American higher education (Hedges, 2009; Schwartz, 1987), the reader might be surprised at the number of eminent scholars who are moral realists. A partial list would include Martin Heidegger (Gupta, 2015), Robert Bellah (Bellah, Madsen, Sullivan, Swidler, & Tipton, 2007), Daniel Robinson (2009), Charles Taylor (1989), Ludwig Wittgenstein[1] (1953/2009), Aristotle

(1999), John Searle (1993), Han-Georg Gadamer (1975/2004), Iris Murdoch (1994), Richard Shweder (1990), John Dewey (1905), Alastair MacIntyre (1988), and Thomas Nagel.[2] Indeed, a recent investigation of contemporary philosophers concluded that a majority endorse the notion of moral realism.[3]

As the variety of scholars on this list indicates, there are many different kinds of moral realists. Even more pertinently, there are a large number of theories and philosophies concerning the general sources of morality, whether realist or non-realist. Therefore, the purpose of the remainder of this chapter is to provide a conceptual framework for some of the more prominent approaches to morality for three reasons: 1) to show how many observers of morality believe these approaches have not stood up to modern (twenty-first century) and postmodern examination; 2) to describe how these problematic approaches are fundamentally dualist in nature; and 3) to situate a nondualist form of moral realism that we believe has promise for grounding morality. We begin by clarifying the nature of dualism generally, and then we provide a running, practical example, which we use to illustrate dualist and nondualist approaches.

Dualist Forms of Morality

Dualism here is merely the notion that subjective and objective realms of knowing are separable and that we can, in principle, understand one completely without the other. As mentioned, many approaches to science have assumed this form of dualism (Slife, Reber, & Faulconer, 2012). The methods of these approaches assume that we should strive to clear away our subjective biases and values so that we can get to the pristine and real, objective world. Consider, for instance, a widely used text on psychological methods by Schweigert (2011): "the results of the research [should be] meaningful, unambiguous, and uncontaminated by the biases of either the participants or the researcher" (p. 2). Notice that this approach to gaining knowledge makes the assumption, though not explicit or defended, that the "real" world is free or devoid of any "contaminating" subjective elements, like human values, meanings, or purposes. The assumption is that we can separate the two: the inner world of meanings and values from the outer world of facts and nature. There are, of course, a host of other factors that facilitated the dominance of dualism in ethics and morality—from philosophy to history—but the influence of these approaches to science cannot be underestimated in psychology.

An Illustration

To illustrate dualist approaches to morality, consider a number of witnesses who see a collision where a truck driver negligently runs a neighborhood stop sign to hit and kill a little girl. The witnesses experience two main meanings in this situation, a sense of anger and injustice at the careless- ness of the truck driver, and a sense of sadness and tragedy at the mangled body of the dead girl. Both meanings or feelings clearly involve moral judg- ments: a young life *ought* not to have been cut prematurely short, hence the meaning of tragedy, and the truck driver *should* not have been negligent in his actions, hence the meaning of injustice.

If you ask the witnesses why they experienced these meanings or made these moral judgments, there is no question that they would point to the phenomena of the collision, almost as if the experience of the event itself prompted them to have these moral judgments and meanings. They might even describe the tragedy as "tugging at our heartstrings," because the little girl's mangled body seems to reach out to the witnesses and pull at these "strings." But does the event itself—the collision and the girl's death— produce these meanings and draw out these feelings? Many psychologists would answer this question negatively. As we will see, most would frame these moral judgments, and even the witnesses' meanings and feelings dual- istically, as stemming from their subjectivity.

Subjectivist Approaches

In this sense, the subjective nature of morality is too ephemeral or too pri- vate to serve as a solid grounding or justification for morality. The wit- nesses of the collision cannot justify the rightness or validity of their moral meanings other than to say, "it's just the way I feel." Within dualism, only the objective is truly real, and so the subjective is not real or necessarily grounded in reality, by definition. Consider two popular types of subjective morality in this regard, individualism and postmodernism.

Individualism

Most psychologists would consider the tragedy and injustice of the collision to be contained within the subjective mind of the individual. These moral meanings are almost automatically seen as private, and thus not objectively "out there" in the real world. The witnesses *endow* the collision with this meaning, consciously or unconsciously. They extend their subjective moral judgment to the objective event of the truck smashing the little girl. Objec- tively rendered, the dead girl's body is merely a mangled physiology, and the wrecked truck is merely a dysfunctional machine. The collision of the two contributes little if anything to the moral meaning.

Presumably also, *different* individual witnesses, with different individual minds and moral systems, would react in at least a partially if not a wholly different manner, with moral judgments that might differ radically from the ones described here. The point here is that this individualist account does not allow for the witnesses of the collision to defend or justify their own moral meaning, at least in terms of reality. One meaning is as good or as justified as another, because individuals can and should have their own private subjectivity, hence their own private morality.

Many important psychology luminaries have informally adopted this individualist understanding of morality (Brinkmann, 2011). Perhaps most famous historically is Carl Rogers (1961) who represents this form of individualism in statements such as this one: "I'm the one who determines the value of an experience for me," not, we could add, the experience itself (p. 122). And many varieties of traditional approaches to morality fall under this subjective category, including sentimentalism, expressivism, emotivism, and individualist relativism.

Postmodernism

An intriguing alternative understanding of moral meanings—a form of postmodernism in psychology called *social constructionism*—is often expressly viewed as *not* dualistic (Gergen, 2009a). From this social constructionist perspective, the moral meaning of any external event does *not* reside in the individual subjectivities of its witnesses, as with individualism. The social constructionist would claim that Rogers is wrong because the individual, the "I," is not the one to determine the "value of an experience." Rather, the moral meaning of an event is constructed by the co-creators of the culture or community in which the situation occurs, hence the term *social* constructionism.

From this perspective, the witnesses in our illustration perceive the meanings of tragedy and injustice because their particular culture had long ago taught them to endow these types of events with these meanings. The meanings do not, in this sense, originate from the personal preferences of each individual's private subjectivity; these meanings originate historically from the literal "creation" (Gergen, 2009a, p. 223) or "invention" (Gergen, 1999, p. 102), to use a prominent social constructionist's terms, of two or more socially related constructors. For this reason, the social constructionist is quite clear that the same collision could have been interpreted completely differently, depending on the culture.

Many thoughtful observers consider this postmodern understanding of moral meaning an advance on subjectivism and individualism (Gergen, 2009a; Triandis, 2018). Clearly Gergen and other social constructionists have questioned the usual individualist approach to moral meaning, and surely some kind of culture or co-creation is involved in moral meanings. Still, does this postmodern account avoid the dualism of subjectivity and objectivity? The answer is clearly no, because the witnesses of the collision still project their co-created meanings *onto* the objective event. If two different cultures can socially construct two *completely* different meanings, as Gergen contends, this "complete difference" implies that the event itself is objectively neutral to the construction, and thus is meaning-free and subjectivity-free. In this sense, the source of the meaning has changed from individual (private) subjectivity to *inter*-subjectivity, but the *objective* event still remains bereft of any moral meaning because it does not participate in the moral construction. The social constructionist, for this reason, is still a dualist because the two realms of subjectivity and objectivity are still separable.

Both forms of dualism, then—individualism and thus subjectivism on the one hand, and social constructionism and thus inter-subjectivism on the other—*ultimately* deny an objective or realist grounding to morality altogether. From either perspective, morality cannot be real or truthful in a conventional sense, and its subjective status implies there is no ascendant morality to judge the merits of the various forms of morality. As Brinkmann (2011) puts it, "all moral orders are equally arbitrary" (p. 70). The arbitrariness of these forms of morality leaves us in the same place—with little sense, as Schwartz has described, of what to do and why. It is all up to our subjective preferences, individually or collectively. Anything ultimately goes, supposedly.

Hidden Moralities

We say "supposedly" because many scholars have noted how both approaches, individualism and postmodernism, ultimately assume moral systems in which anything *cannot* go. Individual subjectivists, for example, usually opt for some kind of egoist morality where everything and everyone are instruments of their own happiness (or well-being). In this moral vision, a moral wrong is to become depressed (hence, psychology's war on depression) or to be intolerant of another's subjective quest for happiness. Yet, questions of moral grounding can easily be asked of the individualist: what if it is not my individual preference to be happy or tolerant of another's preferences? How can you, the individualist, justify your assertion that intolerance is morally wrong or that your individual happiness or well-being is morally right? In other words, there seems to be no grounding for even the individualist's most deeply held sense of morality.

By the same token, inter-subjectivists such as psychologist Ken Gergen (2009b) and philosopher Richard Rorty (1979/2018) have expressed the hope that societies will one day recognize their social construction of morality—their morality's lack of objective grounding—and thus not hold this morality dogmatically or aggressively, leaving a peaceful understanding among cultures. This moral vision is a nice vision, perhaps, but it is still a moral vision, with its own system of values. Again, questions of moral grounding could be asked: what if a particular warrior culture co-created a set of moral meanings that did not include this non-dogmatic peace and understanding? How could a social constructionist justify or persuade this culture of its wrongness? For that matter, how could Hitler's Third Reich be considered wrong from this postmodern perspective?

The point here is that both subjectivist forms of dualism—individualism and social constructionism—are unable to provide justification or grounding for their *own* implicit appeal to some larger, nonarbitrary set of values—e.g., happiness for the individualist, non-dogmatism for the constructionist. For that justification, the dualist would require some kind of *objective* grounding for these moral judgments, yet none is possible in these approaches to morality, because it is located within subjectivity. Psychologists, in this sense, have left the young adults of the Smith and colleagues (2011) study without any defensible morality. No wonder their moral reasoning is "weak."

Objectivist Approaches

What about the other side of the dualist divide—objectivity? Surely, if there are understandings of morality on the objective side of the divide, they would qualify as types of moral realism, and thus be candidates for moral justification. They might, for example, be able to ground the claim that the morality of The Third Reich is fundamentally wrong. Similarly, they might be able to serve as a moral justification for the claim of our witnesses that the collision is wrong. All that would be needed is some objective proof of the moral wrongness of the girl's death or the moral wrongness of the trucker disobeying the law.

Within this category of objectivity there are actually two major sources of morality, one derived empirically and the other derived rationally—empiricism and rationalism, or some combination of the two. Each has its own approach to avoiding subjectivity. Empiricism is considered in psychology to allow a scientific description of the world through its value-free observations, whereas rationalism is often viewed as deploying reasoning powers to discern the nature of reality, including moral reality, without the contaminant of subjective opinion or bias. As we will see, however, neither of them will survive the scrutiny of twenty-first-century criticism.

Empiricism

B. F. Skinner (1971) is a historical example of the empiricist approach to objective morality, believing as he did that his research showed that "good things are positive reinforcers" (p. 98). Bad things, as Skinner further notes, are those things that are not reinforcing or even negatively reinforcing (p. 99). The truck collision, from his perspective, is not reinforcing to the witnesses, implying that the event of the collision is not good for the witnesses, hence their feelings of anger and sadness.

There are a number of problems with this view of morality. Consider as one problem how many critics over the years (e.g., Rychlak, 2003) have noted that empirical approaches such as Skinner's suffer from a determinism that does not allow morality to matter. If the feelings of the witnesses are determined by the reinforcing (or lack of reinforcing) properties of the event, then human morality and meaning do not exist anyway. For instance, a boulder rolling down a mountain may avoid some hikers, but we are not typically prompted to say "good boulder." That is because we assume that the boulder's path was determined by the law of gravity and the terrain, and thus it was outside the realm of morality and not blameworthy. Analogously, it does not make moral sense to say "good person" if reinforcements[4] determine our thoughts and behaviors, and we could not have behaved or thought otherwise.

Evolutionary psychology is probably a more contemporary empiricist approach to morality, replacing reinforcement with reproductive success as the guide to morality (e.g., Hauser, 2006). Evolutionary psychologists justify the moral sentiments of the collision witnesses by explaining how they increase their evolutionary fitness (the likelihood of their reproduction). Given, however, that this fitness is ultimately determined by natural forces that are out of our control (e.g., natural selection), it is easy to see that the Skinnerian moral lessons of determinism apply here as well. Evolutionary psychology also shares with Skinner another problematic assumption for morality—egoism. Just as Skinner's "reinforcements" ultimately come down to what is good for the "I" or self—a kind of ultimate selfishness— so too evolutionary psychology's "reproductive success" boils down to a similar egoism. (Try explaining to your romantic partner that your love is because he or she is a "satisfactory reproductive target.") Evolutionary psychologists will say that such success can account for "helping behaviors." However, they still do so egoistically, with such behaviors ultimately needing to benefit the self's "fitness." In other words, authentically altruistic behaviors (e.g., gracious love) in which the person truly intends to benefit others, even at the expense of their evolutionary fitness, is either denied as nonexistent or declared as impossible.

Another genre altogether for the empirical approach to morality concerns positive psychology. Here, researchers such as Martin Seligman (2011) empirically survey and collect in various ways the subjective moralities of the human participants in their investigations. Seligman is clear, however, that positive psychologists should never commit the naturalist's fallacy of trying to get an "ought" from an "is"—trying to get morality, which he considers subjective, from an objective, scientific study of the world. In other words, his research merely describes the subjectivity of others, and thus cannot be used as a grounding for their morality. This point also means that Seligman's rendition of the naturalistic fallacy itself assumes the dualism of subjectivity and objectivity, but more importantly it means that the findings of positive psychologists are no more candidates for the objective justification of morality than the subjective ones we reviewed previously.

These researchers do endeavor to correlate the subjective values they discover from their participants with other factors such as a person's happiness. The clear implication is that if you want to be happy, you should try the correlated values on for size. Even so, the "should" in the previous sentence betrays some of the hidden morality of the positive psychology project, such as its instrumentalism. In other words, many of these psychologists implicitly assume that it is morally appropriate and justified for these correlated values to be used as instruments of our happiness (despite many criticisms of instrumental morality; see Fowers et al., 2017; Richardson, Fowers, & Guignon, 1999). If, for example, some of the witnesses in our truck collision illustration were to become depressed, positive psychologists might recommend a moral strategy for moving away from this depression. However, as helpful as this strategy might seem to be, positive psychologists provide no moral grounding for their valuing of happiness and the instrumentalism that justifies their project (Christopher, Richardson, & Slife, 2008).

Rationalism

By far, the most important approach to avoiding subjectivity in morality is the rationalist tradition, including such eminent philosophers as Immanuel Kant (1998) and his modern emissaries in psychology, Piaget (1997) and Kohlberg (1981). This rationalist approach is the formalist or deontological tradition where morality is viewed as a set of rules, codes, or principles, such as psychology's own professional code of ethics. Kant, for example, used his value-free reason to discern what is known as the *categorical imperative*, an objective, unconditional moral requirement that should be obeyed under all circumstances. He moved to this form of absolutism because he was dissatisfied with the utilitarian ethics of his day. The utilitarian, for instance, contends that murder is wrong because it does not optimize the utility or good for those involved in the murder. However, as Kant reasoned, this justification was too subjective, because individualistic murderers, such as sadists, could justify murder in terms of their individual happiness.

The categorical imperative, on the other hand, was supposedly derived exclusively in terms of objective reason, and thus Kant assumed it was universal. Kant clarified several complex formulations of this imperative, but one of its primary decision-making procedures is fairly straightforward and even logically intuitive, which was precisely Kant's point. He thought that when a moral action is considered, one should ask the following question: what would happen if I made the moral action I was considering into a universal law? If, for example, I considered killing someone who insulted me, universalizing this action would imply that everyone should kill anyone who insults them. If everyone did this, we would quickly run out of people to kill, and it would no longer be possible to follow the law. Because of this logical contradiction, Kant felt that we have an objective duty not to kill people. From his perspective, the truck driver of our illustration violated one or more of the rationally derived principles of our code of ethics, which should necessarily invite the meanings of injustice and tragedy that the witnesses experienced—clearly an example of a moral realism.

Unfortunately, however, virtually all rationalist forms of moral grounding fail to survive the rigors of modern and postmodern critique. The main problem can be framed as a question—how do we connect these abstract principles to concrete reality? Rules and principles are abstract, sterile, and disconnected from our practical lives, and no principles are self-applying. In other words, an objective code is still without context and subjectivity. We do not live in abstractland, where these abstractions presumably always and universally apply; we live in particular contexts that include our particular subjectivity (e.g., interpretations). A famous example of this problem with the categorical imperative is that of the crazed axe-murderer who asks you where your children are. You could lie, and some would say that you *should* lie, but if you universalize this lying action so that everyone in the entire world lies all the time, there would be no truth-telling and thus no real lying. The universal is thus logically contradictory, and the categorical imperative would tell you that you have a duty to tell the axe-murderer the truth, so he can kill your children. Needless to say, this moral grounding may be fine in abstractland, but it is frequently suspect in the real, concrete world of our lived experience.

For this reason, all abstract principles and propositions from this rationalist tradition can be criticized because they contain no instructions for tailoring them to specific moral situations. What is concretely and specifically right or wrong, when attempting to apply these principles, is often not at all straightforward. Anyone who has attempted to follow "parenting principles" with their children will attest to this practical difficulty. Aristotle was one of the first to note the particularity of nearly all practical-moral judgments, suggesting that the entire rationalist tradition, in this sense, is inherently problematic (Fowers et al., 2017). This tradition would include another form of moral realism, the natural law tradition of rationalism, because its natural principles are similarly disconnected from the context of actual human practices (Brinkmann, 2011, pp. 73–75). Moreover, Drey-fus and Dreyfus (1991) and Murdoch (1994) have argued that morally pro-ficient reasoners rarely need or engage in reflective rule-following. They instead see clearly and intuitively what to do in particular situations. In other words, a well-formed moral character has no need to engage in the moral reflection that Kantians or those advocating a rationalist objective approach require.

Our general point here is the dilemma of the dualist: some type of "objec-tive" grounding appears to be needed to allow for any defensible justifica-tion of a moral judgment or feeling, but without the "subjective" context of the particular situation in which the judgment occurs, this grounding is too abstract or thin to be useful. What is needed, it would seem, is some amal-gam of the objective and subjective, where the two realms of knowing are never separated in the first place—a nondualist form of morality.

Nondualist Forms of Morality

What would morality be like if we did not assume at the outset the sep-arability of objectivity and subjectivity? First, the world would be more like meanings than objects, what some would call a hermeneutic realism where all supposedly objective and subjective things are really inseparably connected—a relational rather than a substance ontology (Slife & Chris-tensen, 2013). The girl's mangled body, the truck, and the witnesses would all be meanings that contribute to the qualities of one another, just like words in a text contribute to the meanings of one another, or parts of a whole contribute to the qualities of one another. From a hermeneutic per-spective, we are all concernfully involved in the world, and so this concern connects us inextricably *to* the world in ways that values cannot be sepa-rated from facts, subjectivities cannot be separated from objectivities. As even our brief review of prominent approaches to morality has shown, sub-jectivist approaches require moral groundings they cannot justify without the "objective," and objectivist approaches require contextual groundings they cannot justify without the "subjective."[5] Consequently, in a herme-neutic approach, moral judgments and meanings—as "subjective" in some ways as they may be—are nevertheless also *real* in a quasi-objective sense.

Forms of Life

How can such meanings possibly be real from a hermeneutic viewpoint? First, it is worth noting that those who experience moral events, such as the witnesses' experience of the girl's death, frequently experience the morality—in this case, the tragedy of her death—as stemming from the experience itself. In other words, they do not report reflecting on the event and then deciding on a moral judgment. Instead, the *event* itself is tragic. The event is not an object, in this sense, that is subjectively interpreted; it is a meaning in which concernful onlookers, *because* of their inseparable connection to the world, *already* have a moral stake in world events. Part of this moral stake involves individual and cultural influences, to be sure, but another part entails a moral investment in life itself. Even if the witnesses never met the dead girl or never thought about the possibility of her death, they are existentially connected to and invested in her living a full life. They know the "should" of this life intuitively because they are living it themselves. Wittgenstein speaks of "forms of life" (1953/2009, section 226e) in this sense, while Taylor talks of "human constants" (Taylor, 1981, p. 205; cf. Smith, 2002, p. 125), Searle discusses "characteristic humanness" (1967, p. 113), and Aristotle (1999) points to common human function.

All of these philosophers are referring to taken-for-granted moral understandings that make meaning itself possible. These human forms or constants are the value-laden facts of our existence. One could, of course, imagine a mental patient or someone from a rogue culture standing over the mangled girl and stating, "how delightful." For Wittgenstein, however, this statement would be considered a grammatical error, because he means grammar as the moral use of meaningful language, *any* human language. Likewise, Taylor (1981) talks about "human constants" that, unlike the social constructionists, would allow a culture to validly criticize another culture (p. 205).[6] An entire culture that delights in the girl's dead body would be morally wrong in this sense. As Brinkmann (2011) describes, we are more intuitively certain that we should help a drowning child than "any [rationalist or reflected] theory we can invoke to back that [meaning]" (p. 3). Although contextual differences must always be taken into account in all moral meanings, so that the universals of rationalism are inherently problematic, these human forms are the intuitive moral understandings that function as vital moral frameworks in making sense of these contextual differences.

The Practice Turn

These contextual influences demand a further development for the hermeneuticist—what some have called "the practice turn" (e.g., Brinkmann, 2011; Schatzki, 1996; Slife, 2004; Yanchar & Slife, 2017). From the perspective of this turn, our lives are filled with meaningful practices, which are situated and shared activities that require moralities for them to work or make sense. In other words, these practices cannot exist meaningfully without moral standards that inform us about how to comport ourselves when engaged in them. The practice of truck driving, for instance, entails inherent moral standards for going about this activity. The dangers of this huge vehicle in relation to the forms of human life we just described imply a kind of moral logic in the practice of truck driving. To even *be* a truck driver—to be licensed or acquire the identity of a truck driver—requires would-be drivers to meet moral standards that are intrinsic to the practice of truck driving.

Moral values, in this very ordinary sense, are real, "out there" in the world, and even constitute the identities of truck drivers. They are not, then, merely social conventions or individual preferences, because they are constituted by the interaction of dangerous machines and frail humans. The world of moral meanings, for this reason, is disclosed through our practical involvement in such practices. The very meanings of our identities are the moral stances we take in relation to the moral ecology of these practices—good drivers, good teachers, good speakers, and good persons.

From this practice perspective, it is right for our witnesses to see the collision as injustice and tragedy. It is not difficult for them to understand that the driver has violated the intrinsic normativity of the practice of truck driving by running the neighborhood stop sign. After all, the witnesses have been drivers or driven themselves. Still, as straightforward as this injustice and tragedy is, the particular context still matters—such as the location of the tragedy, the neighborhood. For example, the witnesses are less likely to feel the sadness of the tragedy and the anger of the injustice if the collision occurs elsewhere and they watched it on television.

Likewise, the moral meanings of the witnesses do not depend solely on the witnesses' culture or their individual preferences, because good truck driving *also* depends on the quasi-objective lethality of the truck, the real skills needed in controlling the truck, and the general fragility of the human being involved in the incident—not only the fragility of the little girl but also the fragility of the witnesses themselves. From a hermeneutic, nondualist point of view, it is the *coalescence* of these factors that provides the moral logic of the situation and serves to ground the moral judgment rendered. And if such practices are commonplace—in the home and at the work site—then this ordinary morality offers a moral orientation as to how to conduct one's entire life. Indeed, this orientation could occur without us even realizing we are oriented.

Brief Preview of the Book

This brief description of hermeneutic moral realism barely scratches the surface of this revolutionary approach to moral grounding. It is intended here only as introduction and follow through on this introductory illustration. A nondualist understanding of morality is not only a relatively new approach to the pantheon of moral approaches, but also a conceptual challenge to the endemic dualism of Western culture. Consequently, the first section of the book begins with three chapters on the conceptual understandings of hermeneutic moral realism. Chapter 1 describes a hermeneutic moral realist position on human agency and participation in moral ecologies. Chapter 2 suggests a hermeneutic moral realist way of conceptualizing scientific practices and knowledge justification. Chapter 3 offers a moral realist way of conceptualizing culture that seeks to avoid the historical relativism vs. objectivism antinomy.

On the other hand, hermeneutic moral realism is nothing if not practical. The second section provides brief forays into how this view might be implemented in the work of psychologists, specifically psychotherapy, publishing, politics, and investigation. Chapter 4 describes applications for psychotherapy, presenting a conception of clinical practice that is based primarily on the ideas of moral realist Charles Taylor. Chapter 5 suggests a view of what scholarly publishing practices would involve from this perspective. Chapter 6 applies the perspective to contemporary political debates and discourse about personal ways of living, and Chapter 7 presents an example of inquiry informed by the assumptions and values of this viewpoint.

Taken together, these chapters offer a glimpse into the premises and promises of hermeneutic moral realism as a framework for psychology. Much scholarly work remains to be done in the development of this set of ideas, and much exploration of its applications for various subdisciplines is needed; but these chapters provide a conceptual and practical sense of what this alternative affords.

Notes

1. Wittgenstein's "language games" are often interpreted as relativistic. However, Anthony Holiday has clearly shown that semantic necessity must be seen in the later Wittgenstein as moral necessity. As Holiday (1988) puts it, there aren't just language games; there are "core language games" that are guided by human normativity (p. 67).
2. Thomas Nagel (1986): "an action can be true or false independently of how things appear to us" (p. 139).
3. Bourget, D., & Chalmers, D. (2013). What do philosophers believe? https://philpapers.org/archive/BOUWDP
4. Quine has demonstrated that the existence of causal laws are incompatible with the existence of intentionality and normativity (MacIntyre, 1985, p. 83).
5. The mind, in this sense, is not a thing that can be localized in the brain, but is rather an array of skills in relation to patterns of shared activity that can change from context to context, as the situated or extended mind traditions contend.
6. Even Taylor's notion of strong evaluations is concerned with such non-chosen moral frameworks.

References

Aristotle. (1999). *Nicomachean ethics*. (M. Ostwald, Trans.). Upper Saddle River, NJ: Prentice Hall.

Bellah, R. N., Madsen, R., Sullivan, W. M., Swidler, A., & Tipton, S. M. (2007). *Habits of the heart: Individualism and commitment in American life*. Berkeley, CA: University of California Press.

Borgonovi, F. (2008). Doing well by doing good: The relationship between formal volunteering and self-reported health and happiness. *Social Science & Medicine, 66*(11), 2321–2334. https://doi.org/10.1016/j.socscimed.2008.01.011

Brinkmann, S. (2011). *Psychology as a moral science: Perspectives on normativity*. New York: Springer.

Christopher, J. C., Richardson, F. C., & Slife, B. D. (2008). Thinking through positive psychology. *Theory & Psychology, 18*(5), 555–561. https://doi.org/10.1177/0959 354308093395

Dewey, J. (1905). The realism of pragmatism. *The Journal of Philsophy, Psychology, and Scientific Methods, 2*(12), 324–327.

Dreyfus, H. L., & Dreyfus, S. E. (1991). Towards a phenomenology of ethical expertise. *Human Studies, 14*(4), 229–250. https://doi.org/10.1007/BF02205607

Dunn, E. W., Aknin, L. B., & Norton, M. I. (2008). Spending money on others promotes happiness. *Science, 319*(5870), 1687–1688. https://doi.org/10.1126/science.1150952

Fowers, B. J. (2005). *Virtue and psychology: Pursuing excellence in ordinary practices*. Washington, DC: American Psychological Association. http://dx.doi.org/10.1037/11219-000

Fowers, B. J., Richardson, F. C., & Slife, B. D. (2017). *Frailty, suffering, and vice: Flourishing in the face of human limitations*. Washington, DC: American Psychological Association.

Gadamer, H. G. (1975/2004). *Truth and method*. New York: Bloomsbury Publishing USA.

Gantt, E. E., & Williams, R. N. (2018). *On hijacking science: Exploring the nature and consequences of overreach in psychology*. New York: Routledge.

Gergen, K. J. (1999). *An invitation to social construction*. London, UK: Sage Publications.

Gergen, K. J. (2009a). *Realities and relationships: Soundings in social construction*. Cambridge, MA: Harvard University Press.

Gergen, K. J. (2009b). *Relational being: Beyond self and community*. New York: Oxford University Press.

Gupta, A. (2015). *Heidegger and moral realism*. Eugene, OR: Pickwick Publishing.

Hauser, M. (2006). *Moral minds: How nature designed our universal sense of right and wrong*. New York: Ecco and Harper Collins Publishers.

Hedges, C. (2009). *Empire of illusion: The end of literacy and the triumph of spectacle*. New York: Knopf Canada.

Holiday, A. (1988). *Moral powers: Normative necessity in language and history*. New York: Routledge and Kegan Paul.

James, H. S., Jr. (2011). Is the just man a happy man? An empirical study of the relationship between ethics and subjective well-being. *Kyklos, 64*, 193–212.

Kant, I. (Trans.). (1998). *Critique of pure reason.* (P. Guyer & A. W. Wood, Trans.). Cambridge, UK: Cambridge University Press.

Kohlberg, L. (1981). *The philosophy of moral development: Moral stages and the idea of justice.* San Francisco, CA: Harper and Row.

MacIntyre, A. (1985). *After virtue: A study in moral theory.* London, UK: Duckworth.

MacIntyre, A. (1988). *Whose justice? Which rationality?* Notre Dame, IN: University of Notre Dame Press.

Murdoch, I. (1994). *Metaphysics as a guide to morals.* London, UK: Penguin.

Nagel, T. (1986). *The view from nowhere.* New York: Oxford University Press.

Piaget, J. (1997). *The moral judgment of the child.* (M. Gabain, Trans.). New York: The Free Press.

Richardson, F. C., Fowers, B. J., & Guignon, C. B. (1999). *Re-envisioning psychology: Moral dimensions of theory and practice.* San Francisco, CA: Jossey-Bass.

Robinson, D. N. (2009). *Praise and blame: Moral realism and its applications.* Princeton, NJ: Princeton University Press.

Rogers, C. R. (1995). *On becoming a person: A therapist's view of psychotherapy.* New York: Houghton Mifflin Harcourt.

Rorty, R. (1979/2018). *Philosophy and the mirror of nature.* Princeton, NJ: Princeton University Press.

Rychlak, J. F. (2003). *The human image in postmodern America.* Washington, DC: American Psychological Association.

Schatzki, T. R. (1996). *Social practices: A Wittgensteinian approach to human activity and the social.* Cambridge, UK: Cambridge University Press.

Schwartz, B. (1987). *The battle for human nature: Science, morality and modern life.* New York: W. W. Norton & Company.

Schweigert, W. A. (2011). *Research methods in psychology: A handbook* (3rd ed.). Long Grove, IL: Waveland Press.

Searle, J. R. (1967). How to derive "ought" from "is". In P. Foot (Ed.), *Theories of ethics* (pp. 101–114). Oxford: Oxford University Press.

Searle, J. R. (1993). Rationality and realism, what is at stake? *Daedalus, 122*(4), 55–83.

Seligman, M. (2011). *Flourish: A visionary new understanding of happiness and well-being.* New York: The Free Press.

Shweder, R. A. (1990). In defense of moral realism: Reply to Gabennesch. *Child Development, 61,* 2060–2067.

Skinner, B. F. (1971). *Beyond freedom & dignity.* New York: Bantam Book.

Slife, B. D. (2004). Taking practice seriously: Toward a relational ontology. *Journal of Theoretical and Philosophical Psychology, 24*(2), 157–178.

Slife, B. D., & Christensen, T. (2013). Hermeneutic realism: Toward a truly meaningful psychology. *Review of General Psychology, 17*(2), 230–236.

Slife, B. D., Reber, J. S., & Faulconer, J. E. (2012). Implicit ontological reasoning: Problems of dualism in psychological science. In R. Proctor & J. Capaldi (Eds.), *Psychology of science: Implicit and explicit reasoning* (pp. 459–478). New York: Oxford University Press.

Smith, C., Christoffersen, K. M., Davidson, H., & Herzog, P. S. (2011). *Lost in transition: The Dark side of emerging adulthood.* New York: Oxford University Press.

Smith, N. H. (2002). *Charles Taylor: Meaning, morals, and modernity*. Cambridge, UK: Polity Press.

Strohminger, N., & Nichols, S. (2015). Neurodegeneration and identity. *Psychological Science, 26*(9), 1469–1479. https://doi.org/10.1177/0956797615592381

Taylor, C. (1981). Understanding and explanation in the geisteswissenschaften. In S. Holtzman & C. Leich (Eds.), *Wittgenstein: To follow a rule* (pp. 191–210). London, UK: Routledge.

Taylor, C. (1989). *Sources of the self: The making of the modern identity*. Cambridge, MA: Harvard University Press.

Triandis, H. C. (2018). *Individualism and collectivism*. New York: Routledge.

Wittgenstein, L. (1953/2009). *Philosophical investigations*. West Sussex, UK: John Wiley & Sons.

Yanchar, S. C., & Slife, B. D. (2017). Theorizing inquiry in the moral space of practice. *Qualitative Research in Psychology, 14*(2), 146–170.

Section 1

1 Hermeneutic Moral Realism, Participational Agency, and World Disclosure

Stephen C. Yanchar and Brent D. Slife

Moral conduct is intimately connected to the issue of agency (or free will) and determinism. If human action is lawfully governed and, in that sense, strictly automatic and machinelike, then no particular activity could be seen as moral or immoral; rather, it would be just what the determinant factors involved (biological processes, social pressures, etc.) caused it to be. Human conduct, in this regard, would not differ fundamentally from the purposeless workings of machinery or natural processes such as photosynthesis or oxidation; it would be the necessary effect of natural laws. On the other hand, if people are agents in some sense and able to act for themselves, then their conduct can be meaningfully evaluated according to moral classifications such as good and bad, generous and selfish, brave and cowardly, and so on. In this sense, agency is often considered to be central to moral conduct: one's actions are one's own, from an agentic perspective, and thus worthy of praise or blame (for more on historical positions regarding agency and determinism, see Kane, 2005; Sappington, 1990).

Like many other positions on morality, hermeneutic moral realism entails a kind of agency; but given its rejection of the commonly assumed subject-object split, as described in the introductory chapter, the agency it entails is unique. Our purpose in this chapter is to clarify this unique form of agency and in so doing, clarify the claims of hermeneutic moral realism itself. As we offer this clarification, we will suggest how humans qua agents encounter the world as a moral ecology, and thus how phenomena show up in terms of their relevance and fit for agents within such a moral space.

The Moral Space of Practices

As the introduction to this book suggests, the classic subject-object split has been influential with regard to how values and moral judgments are understood to exist. Hermeneutic philosophers, however, have called this subject-object split into question, seeing it as one historical way of conceptualizing the nature of reality, but finding neither option (objectivity or subjectivity) to be compelling or necessary when trying to make sense of human involvement in the world (Dreyfus, 1991; Heidegger, 1962; Merleau-Ponty, 1962; for a philosophical review of the subjective self, see Solomon, 1988). The hermeneutic alternative for making sense of human experience entails non-dualistic, fully embodied, lived, in-the-world practices (Heidegger, 1962). Humans are viewed, from this perspective, as inevitably situated in the world itself. No dualism is posited, thus there is no subjective realm of consciousness to be fundamentally differentiated from an external, objective reality. Rather, an agent-in-the-world is a unitary phenomenon of meaningful action, using equipment to achieve her or his purposes, fundamentally with others, contextualized within a shared historical, cultural horizon. Moreover, from this hermeneutic perspective, the world itself is not a neutral, meaningless, and value-free space functioning as a repository of isolable objects waiting to be granted purpose or meaning. The world, on the hermeneutic view, is a lived context of co-involvement replete with significance.

As an example, one does not encounter a particular piece of equipment as a neutral object that must have meaning or purpose projected onto it (or cognitively constructed whole cloth) through one's own subjective mental processes. Rather, the piece of equipment already exists as a useful, meaningful part of a historical, cultural context—for example, a compass for orienting oneself in an unfamiliar landscape—or is invented as the result of a particular real-world need in the context of living and participating with others, for certain purposes. Thus, one encounters a piece of equipment as something that is already meaningful within a context of action in the world, with other equipment, people, and so on. The world, in general, exists in this way. It is a whole configuration of people, practices, equipment, dwelling spaces, and so forth that is already underway and full of meaning. A person, then, is born into this already-meaningful configuration and learns to participate in its practices (e.g., learns to use a compass to determine direction or take a bearing) through increasingly sophisticated practical involvement (Dreyfus, 2002; Yanchar, Spackman, & Faulconer, 2013).

But there is more to participation in practices than the use of equipment in a historical, culturally meaningful context. Hermeneutic philosophers have arrived at the insight that practices themselves, as ways of being involved in the world and achieving certain purposes, must be informed by something not solely dependent on human participation, even human preferences and cultures. For these thinkers, the purposes of a given practice are thought of as moral goods, in that they are the good that the practice is supposed to achieve (Brinkmann, 2004, 2011; Hatab, 2000; Stigliano, 1990; Taylor, 1989; see also MacIntyre, 1984; for a neo-Aristotelian account). Practices, then, are historical, cultural ways of achieving certain goods. For instance, the good of being an automotive technician as a practice might be thought of as maintaining vehicles in operating condition so they may be used to engage in other worthwhile practices. These goods are thought of as moral, not only because they are designed to make some contribution or produce some desired outcome, but because they presuppose values or standards that appropriately guide their achievement. For example, good automotive technicians go about their duties in certain ways, and those ways demand integrity, accurate knowledge, quality workmanship, and so on. In this sense, practices—due to their inherent value-ladenness—exert a claim upon those who would engage in them: to take up a given practice correctly, one should learn, and be committed to, the goods and values central to it.

Understood this way, practices entail moral goods and values that function as practical-moral reference points; they issue a kind of moral call regarding how one ought to participate in a given practice to achieve its goods. In taking this position, hermeneutic theorists hold that moral goods and values are not abstract principles that must somehow be applied in real-world settings; rather, they are intrinsically practical, or practice-oriented, in that they are what make practices coherent and meaningful in the first place. In this sense, a practice does not exist independently first, as a set of neutral activities, and later become endowed with meaning by having moral goods and values brought to it; rather, that value-laden meaning will be constitutive of the practice from the outset—thus, no moral goods and values, no practices. As Taylor (1989) suggested, a lack of such goods and values would be disorienting; without them there would be no reference points to guide what one does. For example, there could be no automotive repair practice without some purpose to guide it and without intrinsic values regarding how one achieves competence or excellence as one of its practitioners.

It has been further argued in the hermeneutic literature that the moral goods and values of practices are ontologically real and actually exist in the world along with people, equipment, dwelling spaces, plans, roles, routines, and so on, because they are entailed within practices which are real, in-the-world parts of human life and experience (Brinkmann, 2011; Hatab, 2000; Stigliano, 1990; Taylor, 1989). This means that those who engage in a given practice, or who seek to learn it, cannot operate in accord with any values and activities they personally choose; rather, these people are called, in a sense, to become like those who already live those values, because those values are constitutive of the practice in question; they are part of the reality that the participating person finds herself living amidst and coping with. Even for a person who does not live up to those values, they are real and authoritative in this moral sense; they are what allow for judgments of "not measuring up" or "doing it wrong" to be made. Put another way, it might be said that if there is no true subject-object or inner-outer split, but rather ontologically real, in-the-world practices, then values are neither subjective nor objective, but real, in-the-world aspects of practices. Practices thus constitute an ontologically real configuration of moral goods and values through which people orient themselves and participate—what has been termed a "moral ecology" (Brinkmann, 2004, p. 59; see also Hatab, 2000; Stigliano, 1990).

It is these practice-endemic goods and values, then, that provide a basis for how one might engage in a given practice and how priorities and desires can be evaluated in so doing. While values as such are not thought to reside in the mind of the agent, from this perspective, the agent does indeed take a stand on them through his or her fully embodied, in-the-world comportment. Goods and values, in this sense, provide a moral orientation that lies beyond any single individual's personal viewpoint. For instance, an automotive technician's personal desire to maximize profit in certain ways—for example, sacrificing caution and quality by working quickly, recommending not-quite-necessary repairs, and emphasizing simple but expensive maintenance tasks—will allow for greater profitability in a purely monetary sense (i.e., what Taylor terms "weak evaluation;" 1985, p. 16); but the technician may eventually come to see this approach as coming up short, in the moral sense we speak of, through its lack of integrity in light of the goods and values of excellent practice (i.e., what Taylor terms "strong evaluation;" 1985, p. 16). From a moral realist perspective, values that offer a basis for making such "distinctions of worth" (Taylor, 1985, p. 17), such as notions of integrity, seem to be intrinsic to the vast majority of practices in which one might engage in everyday life; they offer reference points that provide a sense of what the good really entails, at least in part; and excepting very atypical cases, they function as "human constants" (Taylor, 1981, p. 205).

Human Agency in the Moral Space of Practice

This hermeneutic emphasis on practices and moral ecologies, we contend, leads to a particular view of agency—one conceptualized primarily in terms of meaningful engagement in the world. This is a nondualist view that makes no appeal to inner workings of an isolated, subjective mind and thus no appeal to internal, rational powers that have the ability to act, in some sense, on an external, objective world. Moreover, agency is not, from this hermeneutic perspective, explained by deeper causal variables (as in some forms of compatibilism) or extra factors (Kane, 2005) that allow for freedom of choice, at least on occasion, in an otherwise mechanical universe. Indeed, agency of this sort is not subject to explanation at all, at least in the same way that objects and natural processes would be explained in terms of natural laws, physiochemical events, and so on. While there certainly are ways of describing and explaining agentic human action in the world from a hermeneutic perspective (e.g., Guignon, 2002), those ways are not framed in terms of underlying causes that, ipso facto, become the actual causal reality operating on human beings (Guignon, 2002; Slife & Williams, 1995; Yanchar, 2011).

Based on this hermeneutic theorizing, agency is meaningful engagement in the moral ecology of practices; it is fully embodied and actional, conceptualized in terms of humans doing things in particular ways in the lived space of everyday situations, a kind of situated participation in practice, and thus what might be referred to as *participational agency* (Yanchar, 2011). From this perspective, meaningful participation in the significant, yet quotidian flow of living *is agency*; it is situated involvement in the everyday, non-momentous doing of things in family, professional, and community life, in addition to deliberate decision making. But, as we will clarify, this everyday participation entails an existence structure that differs significantly from what is seen in mainstream accounts of human action and personhood.

One significant difference concerns the role of tacitness (Heidegger, 1962; see also Dreyfus, 1991; Okrent, 1988). While deliberate decision making and problem solving (e.g., determining what caused a problem and determining how to solve it) are clearly a part of everyday living, and thus are relevant to hermeneutic accounts, participational agency also encompasses pre-reflective, tacit forms of participation. For example, a good deal of what automotive technicians do in their everyday work is not the subject of conscious deliberation. They use their tools in familiar and unreflective ways, which enables them to focus on the automotive problem they are trying to solve (unless, for example, a tool is malfunctioning).

As hermeneutic theorists have argued, a good deal of human activity is of this tacit sort and is thus not explicitly reflected on and analyzed "in the moment" (though reflection and analysis are modes of being involved in the world also, and sometimes useful; see Dreyfus, 1991; Heidegger, 1962); but it is nonetheless part of agency in that it is entailed within the ordinary and purpose-filled tasks of life such as working a job, preparing food, driving a car, recreating, and so on. Participational agency thus includes both tacit and deliberate aspects of involvement in practices. While this two-fold emphasis clearly follows from hermeneutic theorizing, it is not included in libertarian or other perspectives that conceptualize agency in terms of detached rationality or deliberate decision making against a background of lawful necessity (Bandura, 2006; Baumeister, 2008; see also Kane, 2005).

To adequately understand this tacit and deliberate agency, however, one must also be aware of Heidegger's (1962) observation that human action is meaningful in the sense that it is characterized by *existential concern* and functions as a kind of *concernful involvement*. The various aspects of human existence that Heidegger phenomenologically identified (e.g., dwelling in a world, with others, with equipment, oriented toward possibilities, and so on) can, he noted, be brought into a kind of ontological unity by recognizing that they all point to one key insight: people care or are concerned about the nature of human existence in general and their own lives in particular. Humans are, Heidegger contends, the beings that take a stand on their own being, or put differently, the beings for whom their own being is an issue.

This concern with being manifests not only in people's efforts to make sense of human existence in general—for example contemplating the meaning and purpose of life, or perhaps more formally, constructing social theories about human phenomena—but also in their concern with matters central to their own situation, for example, the projects in which they are invested (e.g., family, profession, upward mobility, a social cause, a political movement), what they have accomplished, the health of loved ones, and so forth. Even relatively mundane considerations that arise in average everydayness are part of this concern, such as being at a meeting on time, staying within a budget, planning a vacation, or maintaining property. In this sense, existential concern does not necessarily refer to benevolent acts and kind consideration toward others (though it certainly may), but rather more broadly to whatever makes a difference to people in their lives, whatever that may entail. From a hermeneutic perspective, existential concern is a primary feature of human life and agency, as it is intrinsic to how humans participate in the world. And as humans act concernfully in the world, they are taking a stand on their own being.

Although concernful involvement does not necessarily entail benevolent acts and kind consideration, it would be incorrect to conclude that it bears no relation to the goods and values that constitute a moral ecology of practice. Indeed, from this perspective, how one is or can be concernfully involved makes sense only against a moral backdrop of goods and values that provide possibilities for better or worse conduct. Or, it might be said that goods and values provide a sense of what people *should* care about as they engage in a given practice. Goods and values thus provide a context for concernful involvement; and one's concernful involvement is the stance that one takes in the midst of a moral ecology—that is, how one lives up to goods and values, or seeks to balance them, or ignores them, and so on. In this sense, one's concernful involvement constitutes a kind of commentary on these practice-endemic goods and values (Taylor, 1989); and what one does—as a kind of moral commentary—is bound up with who one is as an agent. As Charles Taylor (1989) argued, a sense of the good and a sense of the self are inextricable.

For example, a college professor will go about her work in a moral space of practice that includes expectations (i.e., values and goods to pursue) regarding excellence in this profession. Those expectations—for example, expertise in a specialty area, research prowess, and excellent mentoring— function as values that lead toward the goods of professorship, such as contributing to knowledge and facilitating student development. Individual professors will surely vary in how they seek to live up to these expectations, and how they vary will reflect, at least in part, what matters to them (perhaps in various degrees) in the midst of practice. Thus, concernful involvement, and indeed, this hermeneutic form of agency itself, implies moral ecologies of practice, as these ecologies indicate what one in this position ought to care about; they provide moral reference points that, when followed, actualize the goods of practice. On the other hand, with no moral ecology, there would no basis for concernful involvement, as there would be no broader indication of what should matter to one who participates in a given practice, no basis for pursuing its goods, no basis for meaningful participation, and ultimately, as we suggested previously, no practice itself.

Agency, Temporality, and Morality

From a hermeneutic perspective, and consistent with Heidegger's (1962) analysis of being, the phenomenon of concern must also be understood as possessing a temporal structure. It might be said, from this perspective, that participational agency is characterized by situated, existential concern and that the structure of such concern is *temporality*. In presenting this central tenet of hermeneutics and participational agency, it is important to clarify the nature of temporality (or the phenomenon of time) as a way of talking about human existence per se. Hermeneutic temporality is, first and foremost, not an abstract principle of the universe or a metaphysical force with an existence of its own. Though time might be informally viewed as a force in motion, so to speak, that pulls reality along with it, or as a kind of all-pervasive flow in which events are caught up and pushed forward, hermeneutic theorists have instead considered time to be a description of human existence itself. In this sense, humans as agents *are* time, which entails a threefold structure of past (or historicity), present (or possibility), and future (or futurity). This view is surely radical in western thought, and calls for a rethinking of many phenomena, including human nature (Heidegger, 1962; Slife, 1993; Slife & Fisher, 2000); but, as we will suggest, it also provides an important basis for possibility and thus for meaningful or concernful involvement in the world.

In many traditional views of human action and choice, the past is taken to be a causal force, determining what one does and, in a sense, who one is. Stated simply, from this traditional perspective, actions in the present are thought to be a result of causal historical events including one's own prior activities. Those events and activities shape the person fundamentally, and thus, in conjunction with natural laws, determine everything about him. This is a hard deterministic position in that the person is, in effect, a necessary outcome of history and natural law. Some have distilled this set of claims into the "consequence argument" (Kane, 2005, p. 23) which holds that if all human action is a consequence of history and natural law, and if history and natural law cannot be changed, then a person's present actions and choices are determined by those unchangeable factors and there is no genuine possibility for them to be otherwise. The force of the past, in this sense, obviates free will or agency, at least as those concepts are commonly understood.

From a hermeneutic perspective, however, the past is viewed differently. Instead of being conceived as a force that unidirectionally and independently determines the present, the past narratively "sets the stage" for, but does not strictly determine, concernful involvement in the "here and now." In this sense, the past is in the "here and now," co-occurring with it by providing a meaningful context of relevant events and actions that, in turn, offers possibilities regarding what matters in a given practice and how it might be dealt with in one's current and future participation. This is sometimes referred to as *historicity* (Heidegger, 1962). For example, a college student's decision to major in mathematics education would not be an isolated event, lacking historical context by virtue of which this decision could be seen as reasonable or coherent. And if this student were queried as to why she selected this major, she would likely explain her decision in terms of what matters to her in the present, but also in terms of meaningful past experiences as a math student and perhaps prior interactions with inspiring teachers, family members, and so forth. These prior involvements and concerns, in conjunction with a host of other prior events—for example, succeeding in advanced high school math classes, completing high school, enrolling in college, receiving family support, and so forth—are what would place this student in a position to declare math education as a major. Importantly, this historical context would also reflect what we have termed a moral ecology, as this student would have prior experience in academic practices—for example, in middle and high school—that entail certain goods and values such as a desire to learn, honesty, humility, dedication, and ultimately, the development of knowledge and skill. What matters to the student, in terms of how she previously negotiated this moral ecology, would figure prominently in her present efforts to obtain a math education degree.

One's present actions are thus understood to make sense as meaningful extensions of, or responses to, the context and possibilities provided by the past; and without this past context, there would be no history of situated, existential concern to render present concernful involvement coherent and meaningful (Guignon, 2012; Heidegger, 1962). Indeed, from a hermeneutic perspective there would be no basis for concernful involvement at all if there were no historical events to contextualize such involvement and provide a backdrop of meaningful possibilities out of which current choices can be said to flow. In this respect, it is surely correct to say that history limits present and future possibilities, as not any and all possibilities can flow from a given set of prior events; but it is also correct to say that prior events enable present and future possibilities.

From this hermeneutic perspective, then, an agent's understanding of her possible involvement in practices is enabled by historical context, but also by an anticipated future that she looks toward, and which is informed by the moral goods and values intrinsic to that practice—what has been termed *futurity* (Guignon, 2012; Heidegger, 1962). In this sense, historically informed, future possibilities are integral to agency because they are what an agent may press into by virtue of everyday participation in the moral ecology of practice. For example, a mathematics education student would understand herself, at least in part, as being oriented toward a future in which she is a school teacher or college professor who seeks to achieve certain goods—that is, what should matter to a math teacher—such as facilitating her own students' excellence in this topic area. In this sense, historicity, possibility, futurity, moral ecologies, and agency are inextricably linked. Historical context allows for present and future possibilities, but those possibilities will also occur as part of a real moral ecology of goods and values that the agent encounters and must deal with in some way. From a Heideggerian standpoint, it might be said that agency is a concernful projecting and pressing into possibilities that are meaningful due to their connection to a lived, historical context, to possible futures, and to their relevance within the moral ecology of practice.

As we have already argued, for hermeneutic theorists time is not conceptualized as a determinant, metaphysical force that somehow exists independent of people. Rather, it exists in the dynamic interplay among history, futurity, possibility, and agency. However, hermeneutic thought offers three additional contentions that clarify the temporal nature of human agency.

First, given that time does not exist independent of people, but is bound up in their temporal participation in the world, it follows that the past is not the unchangeable force it is often taken to be (Slife, 1993; Slife & Fisher, 2000); rather, it is best understood as part of the agent and is revealed most clearly in the meaningful ways in which the person considers the meanings of her own life history—for example, the meaning of certain experiences as a high school math student. If this is the case, then those meanings might very well change based on future experience, for instance, when a challenging and emotionally painful learning experience is later understood by the student to be a victory and comes to function as a basis for high self-efficacy with regard to learning difficult math concepts. The student might now appreciate the difficulty that she previously encountered and be glad that she endured it, as it ultimately proved to be a galvanizing experience in her pursuit of excellence as a math student. In this respect, the agent is not locked into one rendition of the past; the past becomes different than it once was. More particularly, her early challenges with math, rather than being viewed as moments of pointless suffering, are revealed as crucial experiences by which she came to see perseverance as good and central to the practice of being a math student.

Second, the past exists only in relation to the present and future and thus these three aspects of temporality are actually not independent of one another, but rather exist as a part of a temporal unity or whole. From this hermeneutic perspective, past, present, and future are not stretched along a line of time, extending infinitely in both directions, but rather exist synchronously as part of the person in her present activities. In this regard, a person's concernful involvement has a threefold structure involving historicity, futurity, and the possibilities they create for present action. How the person is concernfully involved in the world, then, is situated in terms of meaningful past events (that matter or make a difference in one's life), the significance of future possibilities to be pursued, and how the person goes about projecting and pressing into those possibilities in light of their present significance. Moreover, following hermeneutic moral realist thought, those possibilities would be viewed as *moral possibilities*, given that they provide potential ways of responding to the goods and values of being a math education student (or a mathematician) within the temporal context created by the threefold temporal structure of concernful involvement.

Third, the hermeneutic emphasis on the meanings of the past and the future, and on the possibilities that arise in the temporal unfolding of one's life, have suggested the plausibility of a narrative perspective for understanding human lives. As Heidegger observed, and as others have clarified (Guignon, 2012; Polkinghorne, 1988; Ricoeur, 1984), this emphasis provides a unique way of conceiving of human existence itself. Rather than being conceptualized as an object with certain properties attached (as in the Cartesian picture), the human qua participational agent is better conceptualized as an event that occurs between birth and death (Guignon, 2012; Heidegger, 1962). In this sense, people are in a state of flux, growing and unfolding in new ways as their lives proceed; there is no underlying causal reality that makes people what they are "on the surface" so to speak; rather, they fundamentally are what they become by virtue of their concernful involvement in the narrative journey of life (Guignon, 2012). This narrative emphasis suggests that humans are in a continual state of becoming as they develop through life experiences and, ultimately face their own demise as the final episode of their temporal journey. Heidegger referred to this temporal life progression and being-toward-death *finitude*, and it is the phenomena of temporality and finitude that, from this perspective, provide concernful involvement its existential structure.

We wish to emphasize, however, that this continuous becoming and narrative journey are, in a very real sense, a moral becoming and a moral journey (Yanchar, 2016). As an agent fundamentally situated in a moral ecology, it follows that the possibilities she strives toward are moral possibilities enabled by the goods and values intrinsic to historical, cultural practices; and that this striving must be understood as a temporal and narrative striving in light of moral possibilities. For instance, the math education student who learns in order to achieve excellence in her field, in accord with practice-specific goods and values, and continues to mature in her ability to achieve the goods it offers, can be seen as an example of this continuous moral becoming. In this hermeneutic merging of narrative and moral realism, then, one's unfolding life course runs through a moral space and unfolds along moral lines, for example, as one approaches greater excellence through practical involvement, or in other cases, perhaps less so. But in any event, a narrative life structure, bound to a moral ecology that orients one to the demands of practice, entails a kind of moral trajectory; it is how agency as concernful involvement exists in a moral space.

Agency and World Disclosure

The participational agent that we have described—in its ineluctably engaged, concernful, and temporal way of being—differs significantly from the detached epistemological subject of the modern tradition. From this hermeneutic perspective, the emphasis that various cognitivist and constructivist approaches have placed on an internal mind that either represents or constructs external reality, and the logical problems that plague these approaches (e.g., Dreyfus, 1992, 2002; Rychlak, 1991) are rejected as an unfortunate byproduct of the basic subject-object split endemic to western theorizing. More contemporary embodied approaches that also assume representationalism in some form (Adams & Aizawa, 2009; Gibbs, 2006) encounter similar difficulties (Spackman & Yanchar, 2014). In contrast, participational agents are fundamentally situated in the world and thus not theorized to possess a private mental realm that passively represents or actively constructs reality. From this perspective, the world is disclosed or revealed to agents in particular ways based on their concernful involvement in practices, which is to say that entities show up for agents as already culturally formed and meaningful, fitting into a relational totality of people, equipment, dwelling spaces, tasks, roles, and so forth. The agent, then, participates in a familiar world in which he can be described as "at-home," though it will undoubtedly also entail uncanny experiences that, at times, disrupt this at-homeness. As Gadamer (1989) pointed out, the locus of the agent, hermeneutically understood, always lies between the strange and the familiar.

As an example of this form of disclosure, consider an object such as lined notebook paper, which simply shows up as something on which to write, at least for people with the requisite cultural background (which is probably most people). This paper entails a kind of ordinariness and actuality, as part of one's cultural at-homeness; it just shows up as this useful item without careful observation, reflection, or theorizing. However, because entities also entail a kind of possibility from this hermeneutic perspective (Heidegger, 1977a) and thus have no single, determinant nature, paper may show up in other ways also, given one's situation and activity—for example, as material for a paper airplane, as tinder to start a fire, or as a type of blade that can cut skin. In general, how something is disclosed or revealed to humans depends on how they are practically involved in the world. This disclosure, from a hermeneutic perspective, is not a cognitive process per se; it is just how the world shows up (without mental mediation; Dreyfus, 2002) to a fully embodied, participational agent engaged in a particular way. This insight regarding agency and world is sometimes referred to as the "intentional arc" (Dreyfus, 2002; Merleau-Ponty, 1962), conceptualized in conjunction with the notion of *hermeneutic realism* (Dreyfus, 1991). Because there is no subject-object split, on this account, and thus no inner mental space in which to represent external sensations, agent and world—including practices—constitute a unitary phenomenon that includes a "clearing" or a region of "lighting" in which something like paper shows up in a particular way, often as a common cultural artifact but possibly in other ways also (Heidegger, 1962, 1977b).

For hermeneutic thinkers, however, entities do not show up as self-contained objects in isolation. They are configured within a contextual whole along with related entities—that is, as part of an equipmental totality (Heidegger, 1962). Notebook paper, for instance, fits within a context in relation to other entities such as pens, pencils, erasers, desks, tables, folders, paper clips, and so forth, all of which are meaningful by virtue of how they relate to one another and are available for human purposes. The meaning of paper, in this sense, has to do with how it is relationally situated in this contextual whole. Taking this notion further, hermeneutic thinkers argue that this relational whole or equipmental totality constitutes a *world* in the human, cultural sense—for example, the world of the mathematics education major in American colleges. It might then be said, for participational agents, that a world is disclosed though their concernful involvement—that is, a cultural world of human dwelling in which entities appear as meaningful and in which people's activities can be carried out in ordinary ways (Heidegger, 1962). In this ontological sense, participational agents are neither cognitive world representers nor world constructors, but existential world disclosers.

Hermeneutic theorizing (Heidegger, 1962) also suggests that agents are themselves disclosed in particular ways, principally as dwelling in a familiar world that they, by and large, do not create or control (e.g., one does not control one's birthplace, native language, cultural context, extended family make up, etc.) and that is thus part of the actuality (facticity) of human existence. Moreover, as we suggested previously, agents find themselves pressing into possibilities within a world as an intrinsic part of their temporal, future-oriented existence; and these possibilities are projected in the light of an historical, cultural world-clearing that is disclosed through practical involvement. But from a hermeneutic moral realist perspective, the world that is disclosed, and that provides a backdrop for projecting and pressing into possibilities, is a world of human practices that entails the moral ecology we have already described. This means that world disclosure is not merely the revealing of equipment, roles, routines, and so on, but also the revealing of ontologically real goods and values that are intrinsic to dwelling and practices within that world and thus that allow for there to be better and worse ways to engage in dwelling and practice; or stated differently, world disclosure is, at least in part, the revealing of a moral world with real goods and values intrinsic to it. World disclosure, then, is the disclosure of in-the-world practice as a moral space—a claim that accords with the moral realist argument regarding the reality of goods and values and the claims they make upon participants in practices. It is the facticity of practice-endemic goods and values that allows practices to make claims upon agents who would participate in them. Those goods and values are, in this sense, unconcealed as actually in the world-clearing and mattering as one goes about engagement in practices.

As entities are disclosed in the midst of concernful involvement, then, they are revealed in terms of their fit within this moral space. Certain kinds of educational technology, for instance, may show up as ways to make math learning more effective and engaging, or to facilitate the assessment of performance. And in that sense, they may facilitate one's efforts to achieve the values and goods of practice as a math student. Understanding how something like a new form of technology fits into practice, then, can be understood in terms of how it relates to, and possibly reconfigures, aspects of the goods and values of that practice. Of course, these technologies may also provide new challenges, such as making learning more difficult for some and thus functioning as a disincentive, or presenting some students with new opportunities for cheating.

From this hermeneutic perspective, then, it is not surprising that situations are often disclosed as morally complex, presenting people with ambiguities, contradictions, and paradoxes. Given that moral goods and values do not exist transparently and in "pure presence" (i.e., complete and internally consistent; Hatab, 1995, p. 411) within abstract theoretical space, but actually in the world of practices along with people, equipment, tasks, and so forth, it follows that moral reality will be as complex as reality under any other description—that is, filled with the messiness that occurs when real people go about real life activities and inevitably face challenges such as unrealistic expectations, conflicting values, or paralyzing binds. From this moral realist perspective, moral simplicity and seamless consistency are neither realities nor ideals, and moral complexity is not symptomatic of insufficient theorizing. As Hatab (1995, p. 411) contended,

> The value of Heidegger's notion of dwelling is that we are forced to give up the idea that such conditions of finitude are "deficiencies." This *is* the ethical world, and the myth of pure "presence" must be surrendered in moral philosophy, no less than in ontology.

Human agency might then be thought of as concernful involvement, but also as a kind of "ethical dwelling" (Hatab, 1995, p. 411) or moral participation in practices; and as a kind of ethical dwelling, agency discloses a world in which moral goods and values are realities to be dealt with; they are real aspects of the worlds that agents disclose and the concrete situations in which they participate. In this sense, participational agency is a moral agency.

Conclusion

We have presented a hermeneutic moral realist account of human agency. Questions concerning the hard reality of physical forces and the inevitable push of history are, from this perspective, off the mark. While there is surely a kind of orderliness to reality, which can be conceptualized and studied through natural science methods, it is human reality per se—with its practices and intrinsic moral reference points—that is also orderly, but most salient, if everyday comportment is taken to be the meaningful and purposive phenomenon described in hermeneutic thought, and if it is taken to be the starting point for inquiry. We do not offer specific recommendations for research here; we do suggest, however, that these ideas provide the basis for an interpretive frame capable of revealing practices as moral spaces for action. That is, a moral realist interpretive frame can facilitate efforts to foreground ontologically real goods and values, and show their relevance to human action in context, by providing a set of concepts (e.g., moral goods, moral values, moral complexities, moral dwelling) that flow from the basic observation that human action is inevitably situated within, and oriented according to, a real moral ecology.

References

Adams, F., & Aizawa, K. (2009). Embodied cognition and the extended mind. In J. Symons & P. Calvo (Eds.), *The Routledge companion to philosophy of psychology* (pp. 193–213). New York: Routledge.

Bandura, A. (2006). Toward a psychology of human agency. *Perspectives on Psychological Science, 1*(2), 164–180.

Baumeister, R. F. (2008). Free will in scientific psychology. *Perspectives on Psychological Science, 3*(1), 14–19.

Brinkmann, S. (2004). The topography of moral ecology. *Theory & Psychology, 14*(1), 57–80.

Brinkmann, S. (2011). *Psychology as a moral science: Perspectives on normativity.* New York: Springer.

Dreyfus, H. L. (1991). *Being-in-the-world: A commentary on Heidegger's Being and Time, division 1.* Cambridge, MA: MIT Press.

Dreyfus, H. L. (1992). *What computers still can't do.* Cambridge, MA: MIT Press.

Dreyfus, H. L. (2002). Intelligence without representation: Merleau-Ponty's critique of mental representation. *Phenomenology and the Cognitive Sciences, 1,* 367–383.

Gadamer, H. G. (1989). *Truth and method* (2nd rev. ed.). New York: Continuum.

Gibbs, R. (2006). *Embodiment and cognitive science.* New York: Cambridge University Press.

Guignon, C. B. (2002). Ontological presuppositions of the determinism-free will debate. In H. Atmanspacher & R. Bishop (Eds.), *Between chance and choice: Interdisciplinary perspectives on determinism* (pp. 321–337). Charlottesville, VA: Imprint Academic.

Guignon, C. B. (2012). Becoming a person: Hermeneutic phenomenology's contribution. *New Ideas in Psychology, 30,* 97–106.

Hatab, L. J. (1995). Ethics and finitude: Heideggerian contributions to moral philosophy. *International Philosophical Quarterly, 35*(4), 403–417.

Hatab, L. J. (2000). *Ethics and finitude: Heideggerian contributions to moral philosophy.* Lanham, MD: Rowman & Littlefield.

Heidegger, M. (1962). *Being and time.* New York: Harper Collins.

Heidegger, M. (1977a). What is metaphysics? In D. F. Krell (Ed.), *Basic writings* (pp. 95–112). New York: Harper Collins.

Heidegger, M. (1977b). The origin of the work of art. In D. F. Krell (Ed.), *Basic writings* (pp. 149–187). New York: Harper Collins.

Kane, R. (2005). *A contemporary introduction to free will.* New York: Oxford University Press.

MacIntyre, A. (1984). *After virtue* (2nd ed.). Notre Dame, IN: Notre Dame University Press.

Merleau-Ponty, M. (1962). *Phenomenology of perception.* New York: Routledge.

Okrent, M. (1988). *Heidegger's pragmatism: Understanding, being, and the critique of metaphysics.* Ithaca, NY: Cornell University Press.

Polkinghorne, D. E. (1988). *Narrative knowing and the human sciences.* Albany, NY: State University of New York Press.

Ricoeur, P. (1984). *Time and narrative.* Chicago: University of Chicago Press.

Rychlak, J. F. (1991). *Artificial intelligence and human reason: A teleological critique.* New York: Columbia University Press.

Sappington, A. A. (1990). Recent psychological approaches to the free will versus determinism issue. *Psychological Bulletin, 108,* 19–29.

Slife, B. D. (1993). *Time and psychological explanation.* Albany, NY: State University of New York Press.

Slife, B. D., & Fisher, A. M. (2000). Modern and postmodern approaches to the free will/determinism dilemma in psychotherapy. *Journal of Humanistic Psychology, 40,* 80–107.

Slife, B. D., & Williams, R. N. (1995). *What's behind the research? Discovering hidden assumptions in the behavioral sciences.* Thousand Oaks, CA: Sage Publications.

Solomon, R. C. (1988). *Continental philosophy since 1750: The rise and fall of the self.* New York: Oxford University Press.

Spackman, J. S., & Yanchar, S. C. (2014). Embodied cognition, representationalism, and mechanism: A review and analysis. *Journal for the Theory of Social Behavior, 44*(1), 46–79.

Stigliano, A. (1990). The moral basis of human science. *Saybrook Review, 8*(1), 73–104.

Taylor, C. (1981). Understanding and explanation in the geisteswissenschaften. In S. Holtzman & C. Leich (Eds.), *Wittgenstein: To follow a rule* (pp. 191–210). London, UK: Routledge.

Taylor, C. (1985). *Human agency and language: Philosophical papers* (Vol. 1). New York: Cambridge University Press.

Taylor, C. (1989). *Sources of the self: The making of the modern identity.* Cambridge, MA: Harvard University Press.

Yanchar, S. C. (2011). Participational agency. *Review of General Psychology, 15*(3), 277–287.

Yanchar, S. C. (2016). Identity, interpretation, and the moral ecology of learning. *Theory & Psychology, 26*(4), 496–515.

Yanchar, S. C., Spackman, J. S., & Faulconer, J. E. (2013). Learning as embodied familiarization. *Journal of Theoretical and Philosophical Psychology, 33*(4), 216–232.

2 The Moral Hermeneutic of Scientific Justification

Joshua W. Clegg

No epistemic act is morally neutral. Epistemic acts (claims, judgments, warrants, etc.) inscribe standards of right action, both in the narrow sense of defining specific limits on what is warrantable, and in the broader sense that in choosing valid questions, methods, and interpretations, we must always rely on value commitments external to any method. In other words, justification, including scientific justification, is a value-laden process, an acknowledgement that has become a commonplace in philosophy of science (Padovani, Richardson, & Tsou, 2015). The trouble, however, is that if science is value-laden, then good science depends on good values; this seems a hopelessly nihilistic view when the moral is so often seen as purely conventional (i.e., what we happen to like).

In this chapter, I argue that hermeneutic moral realism (HMR) provides resources for a more fruitful framing of this dilemma. HMR moves us toward a genuinely "good" science—that is, a science rooted in historically specific values that are still nonarbitrary and thus meaningfully "justifiable." HMR suggests that right action (or the moral) is not arbitrary nor reducibly conventional, but a real property of every situation. This means that right action is discoverable through a situated moral hermeneutics (through the interpretation of a real moral fabric). Doing "good" science, then, is a matter of finding right ways to act; it is "justification" of (that is, not "warranting" but making just) our scientific systems, relations, and acts.

In what follows, I outline this argument and situate it in the context of philosophy of science. I then conclude with a brief sketch of some important moral affordances[1] inherent to the choices, relationships, and institutions involved in scientific psychology.

Value-Laden Science

The value-laden nature of science (and knowledge more generally) has always been an article of faith in the hermeneutic tradition. From a hermeneutic perspective, "knowledge claims are adjudicated within a social order that incorporates and strives to fulfill a more or less explicit set of values"

(Richardson, Fowers, & Guignon, 1999, p. 154). Science cannot escape this framework of valuations any more than can any knowledge tradition. Of course, this view of science is not unique to hermeneutics; in fact, philosophers, sociologists, historians, and teachers (Pearce, 2013) of science have increasingly come to take the value-laden nature of science as a background assumption in their accounts.

Undoubtedly, the critical accounts characterizing late-twentieth-century philosophy and sociology of science played a large part in precipitating this shift toward a socially contingent view of science. Kuhn's (1970) work, in particular, opened the door to an analysis of science as a social and cultural artifact. Sociologists of science like Bruno Latour, Steven Shapin, and Harry Collins (and, really, the whole field of Science and Technology Studies) have since refined and extended this analysis, showing how political considerations, value orientations and other social factors have shaped the production of scientific knowledge (Hackett, Amsterdamska, Lynch, & Wajcman, 2008).

Philosophers of science have also come to acknowledge the inescapable role of values in science. Popper's (2005) critical investigations of science began a cascade of challenges to the naively objectivist view, reaching their most radical formulation in Feyerabend's (1993) claim that scientific decision making is a heuristic, political, and fundamentally relativistic endeavor (and not a simply or fully rational process).[2] Michael Polanyi (2015) also famously critiqued the objectivist view, insisting on the deeply personal character of knowledge and denying the possibility of separating that knowledge from the beliefs and commitments of scientists.

More contemporary philosophers of science have refined and specified the role of values in science, showing their inescapability in even seemingly straightforward epistemic acts like drawing inferences from data. Helen Longino (1990, 2002) has perhaps done the most to show how intimately values and scientific justification intertwine. Through meticulous and detailed argumentation, she has shown how even the most basic scientific reasoning—for example, evaluating empirical adequacy—must depend on extra-empirical valuations. Even Phillip Kitcher (2003), who has long resisted (or at least troubled) the value-laden account of science, has come to acknowledge that there are no absolute standards by which we can judge the relative importance of different scientific questions or agendas and that science will thus inevitably be guided by culturally bound value orientations.

The Failure of Objectivism

There is thus broad agreement about the inescapability of values in scientific justification, but there is some disagreement about what this means for science. Many take the social contingencies of science to be a limit on any extravagant claims to certainty or universalism, but not as barriers to standard objectivist practices and forms of justification (see Shadish, Cook, & Campbell, 2002, for an example of such an account in psychology). For hermeneutic thinkers, however, the value-laden nature of scientific justification points to a deeper failure in objectivism. Under an objectivist account, values are a problem to be eliminated (e.g., they are "biases"), or at least mitigated. But, if all justification takes place within value orientations, then the objectivist attempt to escape such orientations can only be obscurantist. If values are fundamental to all scientific judgments, then they cannot be eliminated and suppressing them only makes them harder to see and evaluate. Objectivism thus produces what Gadamer calls a "tyranny of hidden prejudices" (Gadamer, 1975, p. 272).

This tyranny has been most extensively documented in the critical traditions. Feminist thinkers like Sandra Harding, Donna Haraway, Helen Longino, and Alison Wylie have described countless examples of androcentric values lurking in the "politics of the obvious" (Harding, 1992, p. 571), hidden behind the dramatized neutrality of science (Wylie & Nelson, 2009). Political (e.g., Habermas, 1971), institutional (e.g., Foucault, 2012), colonial (e.g., Fanon, Sartre, & Farrington, 1963), and race (e.g., Collins, 2002) theorists have shown similar patterns in the hidden prejudices of dominant races, nations, and ideologies. These traditions all point to value-neutrality (and objectivism) as abetting, rather than preventing, the

> constant threat and danger of the domination of society by technology based on science, a false idolatry of the expert, a manipulation of public opinion by powerful techniques, a loss of moral and political orientation, and an undermining of the type of practical and political reason required for citizens to make responsible decisions.
>
> (Bernstein, 2011, pp. 174–175)

For hermeneutic thinkers, then, the fact that values are part of science does not simply mean that we need to be more careful about our claims or pay more attention to our biases; rather, "hermeneutic philosophers generally want to call in question the distinction between 'subjective' and 'objective'" (Richardson et al., 1999, p. 215) in the first place and help us recognize the ways that the pretense of objectivism makes us less, rather than more, responsible scientists. Hermeneutic theorists, and in particular hermeneutic moral realists, point us toward an approach to science where values are not a special problem (i.e., "bias"), but central to science and scientific justification.

Hermeneutic Moral Realism and Justification
as Moral Practice

For the hermeneutic moral realist, the value-laden character of science means not just that values are inescapable, but that these values are determinative of (or are the telos of) scientific practices. All practices

> have certain standards of excellence. They are therefore normative; there are better and worse ways of participating in a practice. Agents who are trying to participate adequately in social practices are at the same time trying to take part in the human goods that are embedded in (or are internal to) those practices.
>
> (Brinkmann, 2004, p. 65)

In short, all practices inscribe standards of right action, including science. This is true both in the "weak" sense (borrowing Taylor's terms) of standards internal to (and determinative of) a practice and in the "strong" sense that to engage in a practice is to take a stand on what is worthwhile. Choices and comportments within science work are thus not just value-laden, but value-driven.

Of course, the obvious dilemma for any who wish to account for science in terms of value orientations is the seeming arbitrariness of values. When so many see values as culturally bound personal preferences—a purely contingent matter of inclination (Bellah, Madsen, Sullivan, Swidler, & Tipton, 2007)—a science grounded in them seems dangerously ephemeral.

> It is only a short step from this philosophy of science to the suggestion that adoption of . . . criteria that can be seen to be different for different groups and at different periods, should be explicable by social rather than logical factors.
>
> (Hesse, 1980, p. 33)

Such a science seems subject to the caprices of fad and so inherently unreliable.

The irony of this disconcertingly nihilistic conclusion is that it owes much to our Western cultural understanding of science—that is, to scientism. Scientism (and objectivism) casts science as a purely factual enterprise, devoid of valuations, and projects this vision onto a "disenchanted" (Weber, 1946) and value-free world. This is a world where we don't know how to make moral choices because there are no real moral choices to make—just neutral causal relationships in an essentially value-free material matrix. Then, when we come to understand that science is a set of human practices with a particular history and enacted through a set of radically variable and evolving cultural institutions, science suddenly seems unmoored. Science, like any human artifact, can only justify itself in terms of a human, moral hermeneutic, something that proponents of scientism have so long sought to characterize as purely personal and arbitrary.

Fortunately, HMR helps us to see this dilemma in a different, and more fruitful, light. From an HMR perspective, values in science work should not be understood as purely arbitrary subjective projections. Rather, they should be seen as embedded within particular situations, practices, and relations, and thus "discoverable"—that is, not just what I happen to like at any given moment, but goods inherent to particular obligations, purposes and forms of practice. The basic claim of HMR is that right action is not a principle within a system but a property of a situation. The "moral" is thus neither "objective"—i.e., rule-based, abstractable, generalizable, etc.—nor "subjective"—purely personal, idiosyncratic, arbitrary, etc. Rather, there are genuinely distinguishable right and wrong ways to act in any given situation, and these are given in the relational and moral affordances of that situation.

In this sense, the various contexts and relations of science work carry with them an inherent, or situational, normativity that serves as a guide for the everyday decisions of science work. For example, because science requires that theories be collectively evaluated, science simply cannot function, cannot be science, if scientists cannot trust one another to report their work honestly. If scientists' decisions are not presided over by the value of honesty (and trust), science as collective knowledge is simply impossible. Likewise, because science requires revisability, the value of openness must direct scientific activity if that activity is to be progressive in any sense.

Under the assumption of situational normativity in scientific practices, then, the soul of science, what makes it good, is a faithful, virtuous practice and not an impersonal method. Justification is not simply the construction of rationales but "in important respects a moral and political matter" (Brinkmann, 2004, p. 69). Thus what it means to justify science is a matter of making just our practices: "we accept our accountability for the values and aims that guide our research enterprise and seriously sift and refine the ideals our work promotes" (Richardson et al., 1999, p. 172).

Justification, then, has little to do with method and "the search for method (when this is conceived of as a set of permanent, unambiguous rules) needs to be abandoned" (Bernstein, 2011 p. 74). Instead, science should be understood as "a form of committed social practice" (Richardson et al., 1999, p. 305), "a coordinated, ongoing activity that instantiates some aspect of a moral framework" (p. 304), and justification as the moral labor of making that practice more upright, just, and true.

The Moral Affordances of Social Science Work

If justification is a matter of virtuous practice, then justifying scientific work requires a textured understanding of the moral affordances inherent in science work. These affordances are ubiquitous and shape every aspect of scientific practice. Before data are even collected, for example, norms about acceptable procedures and equipment determine the kinds of evidence that are accredited (Galison, 1987). In the collection and interpretation of data, lab members negotiate complex micro-politics as they try to convince one another about the nature of theory, phenomena, measurement, and particular observations (Lynch, 1985). When researchers write reports, they are bound by certain rhetorical conventions (Traweek, 2009, for example, has shown how an aggressive rhetorical style was necessary to achieve acceptance in physics). When the time comes to publish reports or seek funding, researchers must convince grant readers, supervisors, and colleagues, journal editors and readers, etc. of the scientific merits of their work.

The entire process of scientific justification thus sits within a network of sanctioned expert judgment, with authority serving as a primary arbiter of justification (Goldman, 1999; Kitcher, 1993). This means that there is competition for expert status (and the resources this brings) and so also credit seeking (Goldman & Shaked, 1991; Hull, 1988), coercion (Knorr, 1981; Lynch, 1985), and local power negotiations (Latour & Woolgar, 2013). This also means that social organizational features of these networks arbitrate the process of justification—i.e., prestige, resources, institutional membership, etc. determine authority within the evaluation of knowledge claims (Shapin & Schaffer, 1985). The practices of scientific justification thus rely primarily on trust and consensus (Shapin, 1994)—i.e., fact accretes when the sanctioned authorities agree to trust the good faith of those scientists properly accredited and operating within the approved social and rhetorical norms of science.

The sociological and historical account of science, then, makes it clear that science grows from a texture of moral choices framed within particular interpersonal relationships and institutional structures. These are the concrete contexts out of which science evolves and within which we can discern, and justify, right ways to act as scientists. Though they are varied and countless, it is possible to very broadly outline the kinds of moral affordances inherent in these choices and in the relationships and institutions which frame them. I will briefly do so within the context of psychological research, focusing, in turn, on choices, relationships, and institutions.

Choices

Broadly speaking, research involves design choices about the domains, theories, and methods of research; practical choices about funding, space, equipment, labor, and organization; analytic choices about the epistemic frames for the interpretation of research and the constitution of evidence; and rhetorical decisions relating to report authors, formats, styles, audiences, and forms of dissemination.

Domain choice ("topic," being the more traditional, but wholly inadequate descriptor) involves choosing a tradition, a history, and a community to which a scientist will contribute. This is thus a choice of both the kind of worldview she will be socialized into (habits of thought, speech, and action; the tokens and modes that grant access to the community; shared problem frames, etc.) and of a cohort (a real group of people with whom she will have to share time, commitments, consensus, hotel rooms, etc.). Domain choice thus inscribes a mostly invisible relational contour—that is, the commitment to a specific group of people and to a particular set of values and traditions. Part of what domain choice requires of us, then, is that we take responsibility for that community—learning its history and traditions—and for interrogating and challenging what we find objectionable in it.

Theory choice also involves specific moral considerations. To develop or contribute to theory is to engage in a moral hermeneutics; theory development involves deliberations about what kind of image a scientist wishes to project on the world, the kinds of prejudices she wishes to encode, the kinds of narratives, identities, and persons she is willing to imagine. Method choices carry even more direct material import. Scientific procedures are social productions that, as Danziger (1994) has argued, become social reproductions—that is, in the performance of method, we are constructing a political system, a culture, a machinery, and this materially re-forms some part of the world, traveling far beyond the laboratory (the most obvious example from psychology is the re-structuring of the world to include self-report as a new way of being and knowing). Method choice is thus not merely a question of "picking the right tool"; methods transform our worlds in concrete ways and we cannot treat them as morally or politically neutral. Theory and method choice, then, also require us to take responsibility, this time for the ways that our technologies of interrogation or manipulation transform bodies, institutions, societies, etc.

The everyday practical decisions involved in conducting research also carry important moral affordances. Funding, for example, introduces formal and informal conditions on research activities. Choosing to solicit or accept funds is a choice about what relationships to enter into and what conditions to submit to. Thus, one moral affordance latent in the funding of research is the duty to accept only those funding conditions that don't interfere with our other obligations (e.g., to transparency or participant well-being).

Research also generally requires space, and to structure that space is to engage in practices of dwelling. To create and occupy space is to make choices about the kind of home one wishes to make, about the contours and cadences one wishes research and its participants to embody. Equipment, like space, is another material constituent of research that expresses more general values. To use equipment is to choose to extend oneself (and other actors) into new forms and configurations. When one deploys equipment, one must determine in what directions, according to what values, and with what consequences she is committed to extending or transforming the apparatus of human consciousness, embodiment, and culture.

One of the most dilemmatic sites of moral decision making in research is in the deployment of research labor. Most researchers benefit from the labor, time, and resources of others and this always invokes questions of power and exploitation. To benefit from the work of others requires us to know, among other things, if those whose work and resources contribute to our projects have choice (genuine alternatives, self-determination, adequate information), voice (participation, redress, respect), and fair treatment (commensurate remuneration without discrimination, intimidation, or harassment). The absence of these (choice, voice, and fair treatment) makes research labor a kind of bad faith exploitation that not only harms others but undermines the credibility of scientific work.

A final practical consideration in research is the organization of a research project, and this involves questions concerning governance (formal and informal articulation of power relationships and procedures for arbitration, redress, etc.), planning (formal and informal plotting of work, equipment, and space in a particular time scale), and tradition (ways of talking and working). When we organize research, we must attend to whether our approach to these questions promotes trust, good will, fair procedures, and just outcomes; whether the time scale of our work and planning respects and protects the needs, vulnerabilities, and limitations of our research community, partners, and place; and whether our ways of working and talking promote kindness, understanding, respect, honesty, good faith, and other moral and epistemological virtues that we value.

Another category of moral considerations in research constellates around the warranting of scientific claims. Though questions of warrant are usually treated as transparently arbitrable in terms of canonical epistemic givens (e.g., statistical significance, internal validity, etc.), there is, in fact, a wide range of possible epistemic frames, none of which can be claimed on purely empirical, factual, or rational grounds. As Kitcher (2003), Longino (2002), and others have made very clear, epistemic grounds are always at least partly bound up with culture and value. The warranting of claims and the structuring of a disciplinary canon is thus a kind of moral calculus. We must make choices and take stands, individually and collectively, about what knowledge should look like and what it should do in the world (e.g., should it control? Should it give voice? Should it redress wrong?). The constitution of evidence in relation to such epistemic frames is likewise a kind of moral labor, a crafting of accounts and cases that involves choices about where and how to look, what to see, what to include or ignore, how to document, etc. Thus at least one duty inherent to interpretation is to examine, rather than obscure (as in objectivist practice), the moral commitments and choices that underwrite all scientific claims.

A final set of moral choices concerns the rhetorical contours of reporting. Authorship, for example, is ownership and so brings credit, resources, prestige, and voice and this raises important questions of justice (e.g., who contributed to the production of a text and who benefitted? Are these costs and benefits equitably distributed? Whose voices are represented in the text? What voices are misrepresented, under-represented, or suppressed?, etc.). Because authorship functions as currency within networks of influence, being an author places us within those networks and makes us complicit in their effects (in, for example, propping up the "publish or perish" infrastructure). As Billig (2011) has so ably shown, questions of format and style are also moral and political questions. They are occasions to reveal and conceal, to persuade and position. When we write, we show ourselves, worldviews, communities, and politics, and so must choose (either explicitly or implicitly) what we will stand for. And, of course, I also choose my audiences and in so doing, I make decisions about who is worth talking to, who needs or deserves the knowledge I produce, the right kinds of uses for this knowledge, etc.

Relationships

The foregoing is only a sample of the varied moral choices we face in psychological research, but all of these (and the many not mentioned) put us in relationship with particular persons to whom we have moral obligations. Research involves relationships with advisers, superiors, observers, and others with oversight; with institutional actors, including those who administer grants, IRB protocols, recruitment activities, research labor (RAs, grant staff, etc.), equipment, technical support, and the scheduling of space; with collaborators, including co-researchers, community partners, and research assistants; with research participants or subjects; and with the disseminators of research, including journal editors, reviewers, and staff, journalists, and policy makers.

All of these relationships require care and moral attention and produce obligations to which I must attend. For example, in my relationships with those who exercise research oversight, I have a special obligation to good faith and honesty. As already discussed, science is a complex and fragile human system that depends on reliable, honest relationships among its various actors. That fragile system is also made possible by those who take up various support roles (administrative, scheduling, human resources, etc.) and the integrity of science depends as much on their good faith and good will as on my own. Thus, if I instrumentalize, objectify, derogate, or exploit those who support my research, I compromise the integrity and truth of science itself. That good faith and good will are also integral to the collaborations that constitute most scientific work; those collaborations will only function properly if I foster cooperative and participatory practices, if I listen, and if I offer care.

The research relationship that has received the most attention in traditional methods accounts is that between researcher and subjects or participants, and for good reason. For most research, this is the largest group of people who will have any interaction with (or knowledge of) a given study. This relationship is also fraught with questions of power and exploitation and can have far-reaching impacts. If this relationship is dehumanizing, juvenilizing, trivializing, alienating, objectifying, or oppressive, then I have not only failed in my obligations to these particular persons, but have instantiated, and through subsequent writing and work, perpetuated morally suspect forms of practice (a sort of self-replicating moral micro-culture). This relationship thus requires not only good faith and care but also a robust set of traditions, discourses, and practices aimed at detecting, arbitrating, preventing, ameliorating, and remediating injustice, abuse, oppression, objectification, etc.

A final set of relationships integral to research are those with the disseminators of research (journal staff, journalists, policy makers, etc.). Many of the same obligations already discussed inhere in these relationships, but there are additional special obligations related to taking responsibility for my message. The forms through which my research is presented do not depend solely on me and so I have a responsibility to shape my collaborations and interactions with those who will disseminate that research such that its integrity is maintained.

Institutions

The choices and relationships that constitute research all sit within institutional structures that also constrain and shape research responsibilities. Researchers work with institutions that hold legal or financial interest (liability, rights to profits, copyrights, etc.), including universities, clinics (or other health care facilities), institutes, corporations, funding agencies, and government agencies; institutions that provide auxiliary support and oversight, including IRBs, funding reviewers, subject pools, labor administrators, and general administrative support; local institutional clusters (of resources, responsibilities, etc.), including departments, teams, areas, etc.; disciplinary institutions, like societies, journals, and conferences; and larger political structures, like governments, economic, and legal systems, etc.

All of the moral considerations already considered can be abetted or constrained by these different institutional structures and, for this reason, responsible citizenship becomes a basic scientific duty. Insofar as these different structures foment injustice or harm, insofar as they impinge on the responsible conduct of science, and insofar as they could do more to help scientists fulfill their moral obligations, scientists are responsible for seeking change within these institutions.

There are many examples of well-known structural problems in psychology (and other sciences) that illustrate how responsible scientific citizenship is indispensable to a functioning science. The replication crisis (Open Science Collaboration, 2015), for example, has turned our attention to the fact that psychologists rarely replicate and that, if we did, we might have a drastically different "canon." Many authors (e.g., Peterson, 2016) have pointed to problems with questionable research practices, like p-hacking or fishing, as well as to more general disciplinary problems like the high risk of false-positives stemming from researcher flexibility (Simmons, Nelson, & Simonsohn, 2011), or the under-publication of negative findings (i.e., the "file drawer effect") leading to systematic biases in the literature (Ioannidis, Munafo, Fusar-Poli, Nosek, & David, 2014). All of these institutional problems undermine psychological science and the integrity of that science thus requires institutional changes to the political structures fomenting them; and these changes are our responsibility as citizens.

Of course, there are even larger disciplinary failings that require our attention; failings that stem from a long history of complicity in racism, misogyny, torture, and other forms of exploitation (Teo, 2015). There is much in psychology's history that belies our self-image as a "helping" profession. I will not belabor this point, but a psychology that cannot be trusted with the welfare of those subject to it is unjustifiable in the deepest possible sense; it is a psychology that cannot be trusted or defended. There are other examples of structural problems in psychology, but the larger point is that each of these require our moral labors as citizens.

Conclusion

I have provided here only a very high-level gloss on the moral affordances inherent to research practices in psychology, but I hope this suffices to show how richly value-driven these practices are. There is essentially no part of the scientific process that doesn't depend on countless moral commitments. Some may find this argument disconcerting, but a hermeneutic moral realist analysis of these commitments shows us that it need not be. We can acknowledge the specific values that drive science without treating these as purely conventional, personal, or arbitrary. Instead, HMR helps us to see that they inhere in our forms of practice and that attention to them can be consensual, systematic, and, indeed, the very heart of scientific justification. Instead of a justification wedded to abstract rationales, HMR recasts scientific justification in terms of moral practices whose purpose is to meet the obligations inherent within particular choices, relationships and institutions. Justification is thus not a matter of defending particular claims but of making our knowledge practices more just. When we justify our science, we are not warranting a collection of propositions; instead, scientific truth has the "nature of an event" (Bakhtin, 1973, p. 2) where particular scientists and scientific communities strive to make moral choices, to attend to relational obligations, and to fashion more just institutions and traditions.

Notes

1. I use the term "moral affordances" to refer to the kinds of moral questions raised and the moral responsibilities made possible (and even entailed) by particular kinds of practices, relationships, institutions, etc.
2. Given their public and rancorous disagreements, no doubt both Popper and Feyerabend would be horrified at inhabiting the same sentence in this way. But in the hindsight of history, it is obvious that Feyerabend's project would not have been possible without Popper's.

References

Bakhtin, M. M. (1973). *Problems of Dostoevsky's poetics*. (R. W. Rotsel, Trans.). Ann Arbor, MI: Ardis.

Bellah, R. N., Madsen, R., Sullivan, W. M., Swidler, A., & Tipton, S. M. (2007). *Habits of the heart: Individualism and commitment in American life*. Berkeley, CA: University of California Press.

Bernstein, R. J. (2011). *Beyond objectivism and relativism: Science, hermeneutics, and praxis*. Philadelphia: University of Pennsylvania Press.

Billig, M. (2011). Writing social psychology: Fictional things and unpopulated texts. *British Journal of Social Psychology, 50*(1), 4–20.

Brinkmann, S. (2004). The topography of moral ecology. *Theory & Psychology, 14*(1), 57–80.

Collins, P. H. (2002). *Black feminist thought: Knowledge, consciousness, and the politics of empowerment*. Abingdon, UK: Routledge.

Danziger, K. (1994). *Constructing the subject: Historical origins of psychological research*. Cambridge, MA: Cambridge University Press.

Fanon, F., Sartre, J. P., & Farrington, C. (1963). *The wretched of the earth* (Vol. 36). New York: Grove Press.

Feyerabend, P. (1993). *Against method*. London, UK: Verso.

Foucault, M. (2012). *Discipline & punish: The birth of the prison*. New York: Vintage.

Gadamer, H. G. (1975). *Truth and method*. New York: Seabury Press.

Galison, P. (1987). *How experiments end*. Chicago: University of Chicago Press.

Goldman, A. I. (1999). *Knowledge in a social world* (Vol. 281). Oxford: Clarendon Press.

Goldman, A. I., & Shaked, M. (1991). An economic model of scientific activity and truth acquisition. *Philosophical Studies, 63*(1), 31–55.

Habermas, J. (1971). *Knowledge and human interests*. Boston: Beacon Press.

Hackett, E. J., Amsterdamska, O., Lynch, M., & Wajcman, J. (2008). *The handbook of science and technology studies*. Cambridge, MA: MIT Press.

Harding, S. (1992). After the neutrality ideal: Science, politics, and "strong objectivity". *Social Research*, 567–587.

Hesse, M. (1980). *Revolutions and reconstructions in the philosophy of science*. Bloomington: Indiana University Press.

Hull, D. (1988). *Science as a process*. Chicago: University of Chicago Press.

Ioannidis, J. P., Munafo, M. R., Fusar-Poli, P., Nosek, B. A., & David, S. P. (2014). Publication and other reporting biases in cognitive sciences: Detection, prevalence, and prevention. *Trends in Cognitive Sciences, 18*(5), 235–241.

Kitcher, P. (1993). *The advancement of science*. Oxford: Oxford University Press.

Kitcher, P. (2003). *Science, truth, and democracy*. Oxford: Oxford University Press.

Knorr, K. D. (1981). *The manufacture of knowledge an essay on the constructivist and contextual nature of science*. Oxford: Pergamon Press.

Kuhn, T. S. (1970). *The structure of scientific revolutions* (2nd enl. ed.). Chicago: University of Chicago Press.

Latour, B., & Woolgar, S. (2013). *Laboratory life: The construction of scientific facts*. Princeton, NJ: Princeton University Press.

Longino, H. E. (1990). *Science as social knowledge: Values and objectivity in scientific inquiry*. Princeton, NJ: Princeton University Press.

Longino, H. E. (2002). *The fate of knowledge*. Princeton, NJ: Princeton University Press.

Lynch, M. (1985). *Art and artifact in laboratory science: A study of shop work and shop talk in a research laboratory*. London, UK: Routledge and Kegan Paul.

Open Science Collaboration. (2015). Estimating the reproducibility of psychological science. *Science, 349*(6251), aac4716.

Padovani, F., Richardson, A., & Tsou, J. Y. (Eds.). (2015). *Objectivity in science: New perspectives from science and technology studies* (Vol. 310). New York: Springer.

Pearce, J. V. (2013). The potential of perspectivism for science education. *Educational Philosophy & Theory, 45*(5), 531–545. doi:10.1080/00131857.2012.732013

Peterson, D. (2016). The baby factory: Difficult research objects, disciplinary standards, and the production of statistical significance. *Socius, 2*, doi:10.1177/2378023115625071

Polanyi, M. (2015). *Personal knowledge: Towards a post-critical philosophy*. Chicago: University of Chicago Press.

Popper, K. (2005). *The logic of scientific discovery*. Abingdon, UK: Routledge.

Richardson, F. C., Fowers, B. J., & Guignon, C. B. (1999). *Re-envisioning psychology: Moral dimensions of theory and practice*. San Francisco: Jossey-Bass.

Shadish, W. R., Cook, T. D., & Campbell, D. T. (2002). *Experimental and quasi-experimental designs for generalized causal inference*. Belmont, CA: Wadsworth Cengage Learning.

Shapin, S. (1994). *A social history of truth: Civility and science in seventeenth-century England*. Chicago: University of Chicago Press.

Shapin, S., & Schaffer, S. (1985). *Leviathan and the air-pump*. Princeton, NJ: Princeton University Press.

Simmons, J. P., Nelson, L. D., & Simonsohn, U. (2011). False-positive psychology: Undisclosed flexibility in data collection and analysis allows presenting anything as significant. *Psychological Science, 22*(11), 1359–1366.

Teo, T. (2015). Critical psychology: A geography of intellectual engagement and resistance. *American Psychologist, 70*(3), 243.

Traweek, S. (2009). *Beamtimes and lifetimes*. Cambridge, MA: Harvard University Press.

Weber, M. (1946). The disenchantment of modern life. In H. H. Gerth & C. Wright Mills (Trans. & Eds.), *From Max Weber: Essays in sociology*. New York: Oxford University Press.

Wylie, A., & Nelson, L. H. (2009). Coming to terms with the value (s) of science: Insights from feminist science studies scholarship. In H. Kincaid (Ed.), *Value-free science? Ideals and illusions*. Oxford: Oxford University Press.

3 Culture and Hermeneutic Moral Realism

Jacob R. Hickman

This volume undertakes the ambitious task of developing a theory of *hermeneutic moral realism* that avoids the pitfalls of both absolute positivism and postmodernism. On the one hand, we want to take moral realism seriously against the fashionable claims that reduce morality to the contexts (cultural, personal, social, legal, etc.) from which moral claims arise. On quite the other hand, there is at least as serious of a threat posed by objectivist accounts of morality that render the moral and ethical in terms enigmatical to real human experience—morality viewed from "nowhere in particular" is not even recognizable as such. There are a number of key issues that this volume takes on in order to clear the ground and lay down a framework for a hermeneutic moral realism, such as explicating what transcendence, agency, and justification would look like under a theory of hermeneutic moral realism. In this chapter I seek to delineate the specifically *cultural* concerns that would need to be addressed in developing such a theory.

Why Culture?

The precise need to articulate a theory of culture that would underpin a theory of hermeneutic moral realism extends from several key considerations.

First, cultural frameworks play a primary role in mediating between human experience and human understandings of the nature of the world, providing meaningful frameworks for understanding reality (cf. Geertz, 1973; Shweder & LeVine, 1984). Both classical and contemporary theoretical debates in anthropology are obsessed with (or deny) the implication here—that we can't have a theory of culture without something to theorize about—a *there* there. In other words, what are we to make of the relationship between cultural frameworks for reality (ontologies) and reality itself?

Second, moral philosophy as we know it is dominated by particularly Western concerns about the nature of morality that emanate from a Western philosophical tradition. This carries specific baggage that other traditions that anthropologists typically deal with do not carry, such as the primacy of dualism (or at least a certain type of dualism, cf. Descola, 2013; Slife, Reber, & Richardson, 2005; Slife, 2004; Latour, 2000), assumptions about coherence (Nuckolls, 1993), consensus (Rescher, 1993), and commensurability (Berlin, 1997; Gray, 1996, 2007). Some of these assumptions have been taken on within the Western tradition, but at least part of the problem is that we need some ethnographic sense of the cultural variations in actual ethical practices if we are to pursue the practical turn mentioned in the Introduction to this volume without superficially delimiting cultural possibilities to this turn. Doing so requires that we address a host of difficult questions, including: What do we make of incommensurable moral practices between (or within) cultural traditions, both of which seem to be rooted in a transcendental notion of "the good"?

This leads to the third consideration, pertaining to the development of the anthropology of morality as a field. While there is clearly a robust twentieth-century tradition of anthropologists engaging in philosophical and ethnographic work on morality, there has been a resurgence of interest in theorizing morality from a particularly anthropological approach since the mid-2000s. At least one major point of departure emerged as an anthropological critique of deontology in Western moral philosophy, and it seemed to many that the particularly anthropological contribution may well be found in eschewing the notion of deontology towards an ethnographically grounded form of "ordinary ethics"—a position that parallels the practical turn in psychology.

I will begin with this third consideration—ordinary ethics and the practical turn in anthropology—and work back to the first—the relationship between culture and reality. By starting with a consideration of ordinary ethics as one of the key theoretical debates in the anthropology of morality, I will address how this debate has side-stepped moral realism itself, sidelining critical concerns that, arguably, have simply been swept under the carpet. After laying out some of these key issues, I will provide an ethnographic example to illustrate what hermeneutically engaging with moral realism looks like, and I will then conclude with some theoretical tools that will help this approach address culturally distinct moral realities.

Moral Realism, Culture, and Human Nature

In many ways, the resurgent emphasis on morality in anthropological theory over the last decade takes the same point of departure as this volume does, debating the merits of an absolute constructivist position against a universalizing one. The particularly anthropological form of constructivism was cast as the "Durkheimian collapse" of the moral and the social—leading to the conclusion that studying social norms was one and the same as studying morality (see Robbins, 2007; Cassaniti & Hickman, 2014). On the other end of the spectrum, anthropologists debated the need to provide a particularly *anthropological* critique of Kantian deontological ethics, which many saw as underpinning (largely Western) philosophical and psychological approaches to understanding human morality.

Michael Lambek framed one of the now primary positions in this debate, putting practice at the center of the "ordinary ethics" position, and critiquing rules-based ethical theories:

> By contrast to those who have seen the substance of ethics as either values or rules, or as the freedom to break away from the obligation of adhering to rules, I have argued that the ethical is intrinsic to human action, to meaning what one says and does and to living according to the criteria thereby established. Ethics is a property of speech and action, as mind is a property of body (or, action is a manifestation of ethics as body is an extension of mind). Ethics is not a discrete object, not best understood as a kind or set of things. Taking such an approach has avoided explaining ethics in universal rational, instrumental, psychological, or biological terms. And while acknowledging cultural difference, it has equally avoided depicting such difference according to distinctive values and thus stumbling over problems of relativism. *If I have advocated the exercise of practical judgment at the expense of following (or rejecting) rules, that is in large part because it is a more accurate description of how we live.*
>
> (2010, p. 61, emphasis added)

Lambek's important move is in the spirit of what the contributors in the present volume are working towards. For example, in the Introduction to this volume the editors point out that rationalist approaches to ethics fail to provide instructions for tailoring abstract ethical concerns to specific situations (p. 11). However, I would argue that there is a cost to Lambek's approach, which goes so far as to apparently reject the notion of moral realism itself. In reducing ethics to "a property of speech and action," we risk losing a sense of the morally real that so many ethnographers argue pervade the cultural worlds of their interlocutors (Shweder, 2004; Robbins, 2004; Webster, 2013). Thus, while Slife and Yanchar (this volume) argue that psychology and moral philosophy are in need of a practical turn, anthropology would be in greater need of a realist turn.[1] While hermeneutic moral realism serves one particular purpose in changing the nature of the debate in psychological and philosophical debates about morality, it serves a slightly different (but no less profound) purpose in altering the debate in anthropology, where culture is a core consideration.

This issue is particularly important when we consider the question of whether there seems to be ethnographic evidence of a universal tendency toward moral realism—in other words, is moral realism itself an integral aspect of human experience? If the answer is yes, then this presents a problem to Lambek's claim about "how we live."

Shweder lays out one of the most lucid anthropological accounts of moral realism as endemic to human nature, which he summarizes in five key observations that can be induced from the ethnographic record:

> 1) Moral judgments are ubiquitous. . . . 2) Moral judgements do not spontaneously converge over time. . . . 3) Moral judgments are experienced as cognitive judgments and not solely as aesthetic or emotive judgments. . . . 4) Moral judgments are experienced as aesthetic and emotive judgments, and not solely as cognitive judgments. . . . 5) The imagined truths or goods asserted in deliberative moral judgments around the world are many, not one.
>
> (Shweder, 2003, pp. 35–36; see also Shweder, 2004)

In sum, people engage in moral action and judgment everywhere, according to assumed moral realities that are supposed to actually exist.

While I find Lambek's critique (see also Das 2012) of a more purely rationalist approach to ethics useful, it is also clear to me that an overdetermined emphasis on practice—which Lambek argues is able to sidestep sticky issues of relativism altogether—has probably also side-stepped the entire concept of moral reality. The problem may in fact rather be that moral reality constitutes a fundamental element of moral experience itself. For all of the problems with Kant's approach to deontological ethics—and in particular his conclusions—at least his problem, his starting point, is one that I do not think we can escape, even in taking practice seriously. That starting point is seeking to understand the nature of moral reality itself, and it is a problem that I believe to be at the heart of human moral experience.

Nicholas Rescher responds to this type of objection to the primacy of moral *rules* with an appeal to rather focus on moral *principles*: "Absoluteness thus characterizes the fundamental moral *principles*, while the variability is merely a feature of subsidiary *rules*" (Rescher, 1989, p. ix, original emphasis). Rescher's point at least helps to clarify one critical concern on which the practical turn hinges. That is, it may be wise to adhere to critiques of the primacy of moral rules, and rather turn to practices. But in order to avoid disregarding moral realism altogether, we need to add that moral principles are *experienced* as underpinning these practices. That is, in framing what hermeneutic moral realism is, it may be best to focus on the elements of human experience (and practice) that are rooted in moral principles as ethical actors experience them, and jettison the emphasis on rules. The thing that is missing in the ordinary ethics debate in anthropology is this precise emphasis on moral principles, which, as Rescher aptly points out, cannot be reduced to rules.

The evidence for the pervasiveness of moral realism as an ethical orientation toward the world needs to be accounted for, but one also has to account for Lambek's (and others') critiques that people tend not to walk around like moral philosophers, dissecting the abstract values of a situation and applying rigorous analytics to understanding ethical problems and making decisions. As Slife and Yanchar point out (Introduction to this volume), the dualistic assumptions that separate rationalism from practice (in this instance) may be one key part of the problem, and the notion of *hermeneutic* moral realism may the way out of this problem. However, if we are to develop this theory of hermeneutic moral realism in a way that can help us make better sense of the ethical worlds of not just the Western subjects of Western psychology, but also the Indian Ocean Islands of Mayotte and Madagascar (Lambek, 2015), Bhubaneswar Brahmins (Shweder, 2003), Thai Buddhists (Cassaniti, 2014), Russian Orthodox Church (Zigon, 2010), or Hmong in Southeast Asia and the United States (Hickman, 2014), then at some point we have to account for the place of culture in this theory of hermeneutic moral realism and its potential to avoid the pitfalls of positivist and postmodernist accounts of morality. To this end, I want to lay out several key considerations that need to be dealt with, in turn posing some possibilities for how to develop a culturally robust theory of hermeneutic moral realism.

To start, the issue of treating people like moral philosophers (as rationalism would have it) or practitioners (as ordinary ethics would have it) can be addressed hermeneutically by focusing on the distinct cultural ontologies at play when people engage in ethical actions or ethical critiques. I have argued elsewhere that, while people are not moral philosophers everywhere you go (although some people are!), being a moral realist does not require being a moral philosopher. Instead, if we analyze the local ontology at play, then an ethnographic unpacking of the "nature of things" often reveals ethical entailments that are built into the ontology itself. I have used personhood as one example of this (Hickman, 2014, see also the following example). In other words, one need not be explicitly cognizant of the nuanced nature of justice, for example, if one maintains an idea about the nature of persons that *entails* that concept of justice. Shweder et al.'s theory of "three ethics" likewise ties these ethics to the concepts of the person that are assumed by them (Shweder, 2003, pp. 74–133). The notion of the person imagined in the United Nations declaration on human rights is but one example of articulating a notion of personhood that has clear ethical obligations built into the very imagination of the entity itself—persons are entities that maintain "rights" that are to be protected. For Hmong, one need not reflect (although, in practice many people do) on the ethical principles at stake in the moments when one does or does not appropriately care for one's ancestors in order to "get" the ethical issues at stake. Rather, the ethical issues are actually "built in" to the ontology of everyday things (see Hickman, 2014, p. 218). *In all of these examples, ethical principles inhere in the nature of reality itself.*

From such a perspective, it would make less sense to separate some of the moral abstractions from the world of everyday practice implied in Lambek's framing of ordinary ethics. A move away from pure rationalism and towards a practice-oriented theory of ethics need not jettison moral realism. Rather, maintaining a strong sense of moral realism may actually better reflect a "more accurate description of how we live," as Lambek puts it.

In sum, the first piece that needs to be put in place for a theory of culture to underpin a theory of hermeneutic moral realism is the analytic centrality of how ontology and ethics entail one another. Interestingly, both concepts have engendered major theoretical "turns" that have dominated anthropological theory in the past decade: "the ontological turn" (see Holbraad & Pederson, 2017 for an overview) and "the ethical turn" (see Cassaniti & Hickman, 2014 for an overview). However, despite several attempts to bridge these turns, no genuine theoretical integration of the two has occurred. A theory of hermeneutic moral realism that attends to the ways that distinct ontological framings of the worlds that people live in entail ethical obligations within those worlds has this very potential.

Another issue that needs to be dealt with in order for a theory of culture to underpin a theory of hermeneutic moral realism is the very issue that Lambek brushes aside, as he argues that the ordinary ethics position, "while acknowledging cultural difference, . . . has equally avoided depicting such difference according to distinctive values and thus stumbling over problems of relativism" (2010, p. 61). These issues can only be brushed aside if moral realism as an element of human experience is brushed aside. Hermeneutic moral realism puts practice and interpretation in the center of its analytic framework, without losing the realism that is arguably so central to human moral experience.

What Is "Real" About Moral Realism?

At this point the reader might ask what, precisely, is "real" about moral realism? In order to give a sense of the "reality" that underpins hermeneutic moral realism, and further in order to articulate why a theory of culture is necessary for such a framework, let me illustrate with a brief example from my ethnographic fieldwork among Hmong in Southeast Asia.[2]

Hmong are a highland Southeast Asian minority group whose diasporic communities span from Southwestern China, to the highlands of the Southeast Asian peninsula, to a Western diaspora after the Second Indochina war. Hmong historically practice a complex set of ancestral and animist rituals that are rooted in what I have called *ancestral personhood*—a model of the person that views one's relationship with the ancestors and one's potential *as* a future ancestor as fundamental to human being (Hickman, 2014). In this tradition, funeral rituals and the management of one's relationship with one's relatives after they die looms large in the practices and ethical concerns of daily life in many Hmong communities. The long ritual process for funerals typically spans three, five, or seven days for the funeral itself, but also continues to include critical follow-up rituals in the following weeks, months, and decades. In each set of rituals, relationships between the deceased and living relatives are renewed and managed, and ancestors are provided for, including giving spirit money and animal sacrifices, providing livestock and means for the deceased's subsistence in the ancestral village. While a Christian eschatology might obsess over the ultimate fate of the soul in heaven or hell, Hmong ancestral personhood obsesses with the state of one's existence in the ancestral village, whether one is cared for properly by descendants, and whether one—through lack of support by living relatives—becomes a wandering, destitute, vagrant spirit. Hmong whom I encountered in fieldwork even anticipate their funerals and future existence as an ancestor while they are living, in many cases preparing the clothes that they are to wear when they are buried.

At one funeral during my fieldwork in Thailand, a scandal emerged when it was discovered that the deceased, a woman whose family I had come to know well, had left a written note for her husband in the funeral clothes that had been prepared for her burial. It was clear that the intent was for the husband to discover this note during funeral preparations. This woman was the first wife in a polygynous family, and she had felt abandoned by her husband once he took up a second wife. While polygyny is historically common in Hmong society in Southeast Asia (although not normative—about 10% of households in this particular community were polygynous), in communities where I have worked, people who accept polygyny as a practice generally asserted that the same expectations of marital support and devotion ought to endure between a husband and all of his wives in polygynous families. When the husband fails to remain committed to both wives, such behavior was commonly condemned as de facto "cheating" and an ultimate abandonment of the husband's marital obligations. Both the family and the broader community seemed to agree that this was the case in this particular marriage. The note left by the deceased elder wife laid out these details, describing her abandonment, and condemning the husband for not taking care of her and failing in his duty after he took his second wife. The letter further detailed a poignant and final plea for the husband to make final restitution to her in death—in a way that he consistently failed to in life—by personally killing the two cows that would be sacrificed for her on the final day of her funeral just prior to her burial. This sacrificial task would typically be performed by someone with the ritual training and skill to effectively kill the animals with minimal suffering. Crucially, this moment of sacrificing cows for the deceased is a ritual climax and symbolically central to the support offered by living relatives to the newly honored ancestor, and the number of cows sacrificed is directly proportional to the status and importance of the deceased. The spirits of the cows become the livestock of the new ancestor, forming the foundation for their subsistence as they make their new life in the ancestral village. The wife's plea for her husband to personally perform this act—symbolically carrying out this central act of spiritual support for her—was a surprising revelation, and, in the context of his effective abandonment of her, a moving request. At the same time, the discovery of the letter was (perhaps intentionally) also a public recognition of his lack of support for his now-deceased wife, and as such, represented a significant loss of face to him. Gossip at the funeral was rampant about what would happen on the final day, with speculation as to whether he would fulfill this request from his wife, as fulfilling the request would represent an admission of the existence of the letter and even potential admission of his abandonment of his marital obligations.

With no small amount of anticipation as to what would happen, the funeral carried on for several days, and the letter and its contents were a regular topic of discussion, up until the final sacrifice on the day of her burial. When the time arrived for the central sacrifice, onlookers, including myself, were ultimately not surprised to find the regular ritual expert—not the husband—to be the one who wielded the blunt end of the axe and to render the cows unconscious to sacrifice them to the wife. The ritual sacrifice proceeded as if the request was never made. My friends and acquaintances (including members of the family) largely condemned the husband's failure to perform the sacrifice himself, even despite the substantial loss of face that this would have represented to him.

This episode is useful in delineating how hermeneutic moral realism can help us to see the ethical "stuff" of the situation, juxtaposed against both an objectivist realism and a constructivist, anti-realist account. On the one hand, it is clear that this example is fraught with moral considerations, and that these moral considerations are deeply intertwined with the ontological considerations in this episode, including at least some ontological considerations that are unique to Hmong cultural understandings of what these things *mean*. For example, if the wife really *has* become an ancestor, and if her relationship with her living descendants (including her husband) really *does* hinge on her descendants' support for her, then this omission of sacrifice becomes a much deeper moral transgression than it would be if these ideas about ancestral personhood were merely symbolic. It is also clear that Hmong expectations and social norms about family life, roles, expectations, and such are deeply tied up in the ethical considerations of this episode. In a word, the ethical principles at stake cannot be divorced from particularly Hmong understandings about kinship, personhood, and the nature of the (moral) universe. While an objectivist approach would represent a futile attempt to treat these issues in a cultural vacuum, through a hermeneutic approach one can fully consider the ethical issues at stake and comprehend their gravity.

On the other hand, it would also be a mistake to reduce this episode to *mere* interpretation, concluding that these ethical concerns evaporate outside of the very precise cultural or social context in which they were constructed. In order to understand the "realism" underpinning a hermeneutic moral realist approach to this example, one must consider the particular elements of the situation that cannot be reduced to mere interpretation. While interpretations matter, there are aspects of situations like this one that "push back" against our experience of them—things that clearly do not evaporate when the interpretive frame fundamentally changes. Three examples of such "real" aspects of this situation (there are surely others) may include: 1) the finality of death; 2) the "push" of the other against the self; and 3) rationally accessible and recognizable principles underlying moral assessments. Let me briefly address each element in turn.

1. While different cultural frameworks might imagine death to represent different sorts of change, the finality of death itself cannot be interpreted out of the situation. There is no getting around the fact that *some* corporeal transformation has genuinely occurred. In this Hmong case, finality means a fundamental transition of the deceased person's status from living relative to ancestor, changing their relationship to the living and fundamentally changing the ways that the living communicate with and relate to them.

2. There is also a fundamental friction that we experience in our engagement with other persons. "At the heart of morality lies *benevolence*—a due care for the interests of people-in-general" (Rescher, 1989, p. 6). The wants, feelings, intentions, words, wishes, and admonitions of the other call on us and force us to engage with them, and we cannot simply imagine them away, even if the *way* that we imagine them may affect what moral conclusions we draw from these interactions with the other. In this situation, the calling out of the husband's failure to fulfill

his duty and the call for him to make restitution for them is not something that an interpretive framework can make magically evaporate.

3. As in the truck driver example laid out in the Introduction to this vol-
    ume, while a Hmong interpretation of the situation might emphasize
    particular moral principle and cast them in a particular light, there are
    also core principles at stake—something along the line of "human con-
    stants" (Taylor, 1997), non-uniform universals (Shweder, 1990), or
    "moral absolutes" (Rescher, 1989)—that lie at the heart of the episode.
    Examples of these self-evident truths may include ideas like "treating
    like cases alike" or "protecting the vulnerable" or "justice" all impinge
    on our moral assessments of this situation. Among other things, the
    mere ability of others to recognize the ethical stuff of the situation—
    even without fully comprehending the ontological frameworks in
    which the ethical judgments are being made—gives some evidence of
    the fundamental nature of the ethical concerns at stake.

To be clear, this is not to say that each of these "real" elements do not
require interpretation (ethical or otherwise) as we engage with them. At the
same time—and what is critical for a hermeneutical moral realist analysis
of this situation—these elements that "push back" against us, *are not reducible* to interpretation. It is absolutely the case that the finality of death looks
one way when inflected through a Hmong ontology of personhood, and quite
another when inflected through a secular humanist, Christian, Buddhist, or
any other lens. At the same time, there are conditions of this finality that cannot be reduced to interpretations or be fundamentally changed by interpretive
will. Hmong are not *simply* interpreting the deceased to no longer be with us
in the same way that the person was prior to their death. Admittedly, this is an
interpreted reality; it is also a practical reality—it is not an objective reality in
terms of being free of these constraints, but it is, nevertheless, a reality. The
finality of death, the push of the other against the self, ethical (albeit non-
uniform) universals all lie at the heart of the reality of this situation, providing
a friction that delimits interpretation, without positively determining interpretive possibilities.

Similar to the example concerning the truck driver and the girl laid out
in the Introduction to this volume, this Hmong example illustrates a set of
issues that highlights the nature of "reality" in hermeneutic moral realism,
but it also highlights the need to consider the particularly *cultural* concerns
at stake in hermeneutically engaging with the moral realism of the situation.
There is a durable quality to real situations like these, and yet, fundamental moral disagreement between well-meaning, rational people is also an
enduring aspect of moral life. What are we to make of the fact that ethical
realities seem to be simultaneously durable and culturally variable?

Pluralism and Hermeneutic Moral Realism

Having established the need to understand moral realism as integral to human experience (the first section), and having demonstrated some sense of what moral realism is (the last section), I will conclude by suggesting some of the strategies that can help address the inevitable incommensurabilities that arise between (and within) moral realities.

I suppose that we could debate about "the facts of the matter," such as whether Hmong or Urapmin (Robbins, 2004) values—and the moral realities that they represent—really *are* distinct from our own, which essentially boils down to a debate about whether cultural differences "run deep" or constitute superficial icing on a deeper universal human cake. But at least some of these moral confrontations would constitute real friction that must be dealt with at some level, and as such would represent elements of reality that one bumps up against in a *real* way. Three pluralists have addressed these issues in substantive ways, all of which I think can productively contribute to a culturally robust hermeneutic approach to moral realism— Nicholas Rescher, Isaiah Berlin, and Richard Shweder.

Rescher

While maintaining an ardent moral realist stance, philosopher Nicholas Rescher has also provided one of the most important critiques of rationalist views of morality that, out of vain utopian ambitions, seek to find the end-all-be-all rational argument to unify all possible ethical values. His critique first points out the necessity of a vertical integration from values to practice, which is critical for thinking through both the hermeneutic *and* realist aspects of moral experience. "Rationality is a matter of appropriate alignment all along the line—not just choices with preferences but of preferences with evaluations and of evaluations with values" (1988, p. 115). Rescher's point captures a sense of rational practice that must include a sense of moral reality, but it is not reducible to an abstract, perfect set of ideals.

Critically, for Rescher, rational action does not take on a single form, and he writes against the idea that rational tendencies necessarily lead to a convergence in moral evaluation. In *Pluralism*, Rescher pursues a version of moral realism that seeks to avoid the same polar extremes laid out in the Introduction to this volume:

> For much of the history of Western philosophy, consensus—uniformity of belief and evaluation—has been viewed as a desideratum whose ultimate realization can be taken as assured. . . . The aim of this book is to criticize this idea and to argue the case for abandoning the traditional

endorsement of the centrality of consensus. . . . Accordingly, the stance advocated here is a pluralism that rejects both indifferentist relativism and dogmatic absolutism. . . . Above all, the consensus-downgrading position articulated here opposes a utopianism that looks to a uniquely perfect social order that would prevail under ideal conditions. Instead, it looks to incremental improvements within the framework of arrangements that none of us will deem perfect but that all of us 'can live with.'

(1993, pp. 1, 4)

Rescher's pluralism allows a hermeneutic, practice-oriented approach to moral reality to free itself from the necessities of agreement. His thorough critique of the presumed importance of consensus in moral philosophy brings us closer to the lived reality of ethical life, while still maintaining a sense of moral reality. Rescher (1989) grounds this reality in benevolence and other unavoidable concerns similar to those laid out in the previous Hmong example.

Berlin

Isaiah Berlin's moral philosophy provides a distinct take on pluralism from Rescher's, but one that pushes more directly towards dealing with *culturally* distinct imaginations of moral reality. Berlin called into question the necessity of commensurability of values themselves, attacking another key assumption that (largely rationalist) moral philosophers have tended to make about moral reality. While Rescher questioned the primacy of consensus about the nature of moral reality, Berlin forces us to ask whether or not moral reality itself is more complicated than we have assumed.

Berlin's philosophy takes moral reality as given, arguing that "there is a world of objective values." His clarification is more friendly to a hermeneutic approach, "by this I mean those ends that men pursue for their own sakes, to which other things are means" (1997, p. 9). Critically, Berlin is attempting to rescue moral realism from rational idealists, and his key point of departure is to argue that competing values, while clearly good in their own right, and recognizable by others (even those who choose not to adopt them) as good, need *not* be commensurable with one another. Berlin's pluralism pushes toward a pragmatic world of practice, wherein we must potentially admit that the fabric of moral reality itself is complicated, riddled with incommensurabilities. The key is to develop forms of practice that account for this incommensurability:

Of course social and political collisions will take place; the mere conflict of positive values alone makes this unavoidable. Yet they can, I believe, be minimised by promoting and preserving an uneasy equilibrium, which is constantly threatened and in constant need of repair—that alone, I repeat, is the precondition for decent societies and morally acceptable behaviour, otherwise we are bound to lose our way.

(1997, p. 16)

Critically, Isaiah Berlin's assault on idealism (see also Gray, 1996, 2007) is not only useful in establishing hermeneutic moral realism as a framework, but it further helps us develop a form of moral practice that deals with the specific problems presented by culturally distinct moral realities. Both Rescher's critique of consensus and Berlin's critique of commensurability push us towards a form of hermeneutic moral realism that can substantively deal with moral conflicts that arise in intercultural moral practice.

Shweder

While hermeneutic moral realism reacts against a rationalist account of morality that relies on subject-object dualism (see Slife & Yanchar, this volume), rationality is still important (per Rescher), even if no grand consensus can be expected. What's more, it may well be that the moral reality is more complicated than Western rationalists have assumed (per Berlin). Both of these accounts point away from pure rationalism and towards context—and *culture is a particularly important type of context*, given the way that ontological and ethical frameworks are so inextricably linked to cultural frameworks (see Shweder & LeVine, 1984). It is in this context that Richard Shweder's approach is most instructive.

Shweder's response to this problem is to assert a pluralist position of "universalism without the uniformity" (see Shweder, 2003, p. 38; Cassaniti & Menon, 2017). What Shweder means by this is that the moral realities that people inhabit need to be distinguished from an "anything goes" relativism in which any value can be asserted to be a morally legitimate one. The universalism here comes in asserting a universal human capacity to recognize and comprehend goodness (e.g., the human constants that Charles Taylor refers to). Shweder denies a rejection of the law of non-contradiction, for example (Shweder, 2016), and stands with Rescher in supporting a rational basis for human thought. However, the problem comes in the fact that "there are universally binding values, just too many of them" (2003, p. 38), which underpins Shweder's rejection of uniformity. With Berlin, Shweder stands on the side of moral reality itself being complicated, such that competing moral practices may be mutually justifiable, while also being potentially incommensurable with one another.

It is critical that pluralism not be reduced to relativism. Hermeneutic moral realism is distinguishable because it is *interpretive*, but still rooted in *realism*, and as I have argued above, what makes these realities real are the inescapable elements of them that cannot be interpreted away—they cannot be denied by abject relativist reductions of all ethics to the contexts from which they hail. However, both the presence of interpretation and the possibility of ultimate incommensurability suggest that disagreement and dissensus (and, for the present chapter in particular, *cross-cultural* disagreement) will be inevitable features of moral realities. In other words, just because a set of human constants can be recognized as legitimately moral, it does not follow that these and only these particular moral goods would be supremely valued by all people in the same way.

Conclusion

Berlin, Rescher, and Shweder draw slightly different conclusions regarding the root of genuine moral disagreement. While Rescher "defend[s] the view that morality makes certain binding claims on all rational agents" (1989, p. ix), dissensus is rooted in the fact that moral principles are always interpretively underdetermining of moral conclusions in different contexts—the devil is always in the details. Berlin emphasizes that disagreement may be rooted in the fact that rationally binding moral principles themselves may be genuinely incommensurable, despite the fact that competing values are all *recognizable* as moral. Shweder's "universalism without the uniformity" ties both insights together with specific regards to cultural visions of the good life, and Shweder explicitly theorizes distinct, competing, yet universal ethics that can take on dramatically distinct cultural manifestations.

This leads to two potential levels at which a genuine moral disagreement could occur, barring irrationality. First, disagreement may occur when two rational agents might disagree on ontological principles—what counts as what—without disagreeing on the particular values at stake. For example, the abortion debate in the United States, Ireland, and many other places arguably hinges primarily on ontological models of personhood, and at what point "inert" matter (sperm, un/fertilized eggs, etc.) become a person. Again, however, these ontological elements have clear and unavoidable ethical entailments, as I have argued previously. Second, disagreement may also be founded in a confrontation of values themselves, with no clear path to settling the matter by an appeal to supreme rationality. Some genuine disagreements may hinge on the fact that both agents are grounding their moral positions or practices in rationally distinct values that themselves are genuinely incommensurable. An example might be diverging valuations of competing ethics such as community or autonomy (Shweder, 2003, pp. 74–133). Of course, one of the parties could also simply be wrong.

Beyond providing a theoretical means for dealing with dramatically vary-ing notions of moral reality that we might encounter in different cultural contexts, what this synthesis of Rescher, Berlin, and Shweder ultimately offers is a framework for actual practice in cross-cultural encounters. Berlin admits that this solution is perhaps not so flashy as a utopian account where everyone's problems will eventually be solved, but in the end, the prescrip-tion for moral practice is to take the moral action of the other seriously. Shweder's "universalism without the uniformity" calls us to engage in attempts to understand and rationally grasp the moral reality of the cultural other. However—and critically—none of these problems are to be taken as the conclusion that a moral reality does not exist, or that it can be anything one wants it to be. Rather, these are merely features of the messiness that one encounters when one engages in actual moral practice.

Let me conclude with two critical points. First, only by treating these moral realities *as* realities can we treat these concerns about incommensu-rability and understanding with the same seriousness that those who inhabit these worlds do. Second, it is critical to note that it is not always the case that some rationally defensible moral principle will underpin every position taken. In fact, as opposed to a constructivist position, hermeneutic moral realism has to be open to the reality of evil as much as it is open to the real-ity of good. It may be that, in the situation of the Hmong funeral described above, the husband is simply wrong in his actions, no matter what argu-ments he musters to justify them.

Notes

1. This is, at least in part, what the "ontological turn" is about. This is not to say that anthropologists themselves are not moral realists—they absolutely are. However, getting anthropologists to own their moral realism is an interestingly sticky topic, and one for another essay.
2. This example comes from research supported by a National Science Foundation Doctoral Dissertation Improvement Grant [No. BCS-0852593].

References

Berlin, I. (1997). The pursuit of the ideal. In H. Hardy & R. Hausheer (Eds.), *The proper study of mankind: An anthology of essays* (pp. 1–16). New York: Farrar, Straus and Giroux.

Cassaniti, J. L. (2014). Moralizing emotion: A breakdown in Thailand. *Anthropo-logical Theory, 14*(3), 280–300.

Cassaniti, J. L., & Hickman, J. R. (2014). New directions in the anthropology of moral-ity. *Anthropological Theory, 14*(3), 251–262. doi:10.1177/1463499614534371

Cassaniti, J. L., & Menon, U. (Eds.). (2017). *Universalism without the uniformity: Explorations in mind and culture.* Chicago: University of Chicago Press.

Das, V. (2012). Ordinary ethics. In D. Fassin (Ed.), *A companion to moral anthropology*. Hoboken, NJ: Wiley-Blackwell.

Descola, P. (2013). *Beyond nature and culture*. Chicago: University of Chicago Press.

Geertz, C. (1973). The impact of the concept of culture on the concept of man. In *The interpretation of cultures* (pp. 33–54). New York: Basic Books.

Gray, J. (1996). *Isaiah Berlin*. Princeton, NJ: Princeton University Press.

Gray, J. (2007). *Black mass: Apocalyptic religion and the Death of Utopia*. New York: Farrar, Straus and Giroux.

Hickman, J. R. (2014). Ancestral personhood and moral justification. *Anthropological Theory, 14*(3), 317–335. doi:10.1177/1463499614534553

Holbraad, M., & Pedersen, M. A. (2017). *The ontological turn: An anthropological exposition*. Cambridge, MA: Cambridge University Press.

Lambek, M. (2010). Toward an ethics of the act. In M. Lambek (Ed.), *Ordinary ethics: Anthropology, language, and action* (pp. 39–63). New York: Fordham University Press.

Lambek, M. (2015). The hermeneutics of ethical encounters: Between traditions and practice. *HAU: Journal of Ethnographic Theory, 5*(2), 227–250.

Latour, B. (2000). *We have never been modern*. Harlow, Essex: Pearson Education.

Nuckolls, C. W. (1993). The anthropology of explanation. *Anthropological Quarterly, 66*(1), 1–21.

Rescher, N. (1988). *Rationality: A philosophical inquiry into the nature and the rationale of reason*. Oxford: Clarendon Press.

Rescher, N. (1989). *Moral absolutes: An essay on the nature and rationale of morality*. New York and Bern: Peter Lang.

Rescher, N. (1993). *Pluralism: Against the demand for consensus*. Oxford: Clarendon Press.

Robbins, J. (2004). *Becoming sinners: Christianity and moral torment in a Papua new Guinea society*. Berkeley, CA: University of California Press.

Robbins, J. (2007). Between reproduction and freedom: Morality, value, and radical cultural change. *Ethnos: Journal of Anthropology, 72*(3), 293–314.

Shweder, R. A. (1990). Ethical relativism: Is there a defensible version? *Ethos, 18*(2), 205–218.

Shweder, R. A. (2003). *Why do men barbecue? Recipes for Cultural Psychology*. Cambridge, MA: Harvard University Press.

Shweder, R. A. (2004). Moral realism without the ethnocentrism: Is it just a list of empty truisms? In A. Sajó (Ed.), *Human rights with modesty: The problem of universalism* (pp. 65–102). Leiden and Boston: Martinus Nijhoff Publishers.

Shweder, R. A. (2016). Living by means of the law of non-contradiction. *HAU: Journal of Ethnographic Theory, 6*(1), 8–13.

Shweder, R. A., & LeVine, R. A. (Eds.). (1984). *Culture theory: Essays on mind, self, and emotion*. Cambridge and New York: Cambridge University Press.

Slife, B. D. (2004). Theoretical challenges to therapy practice and research: The constraint of naturalism. In M. J. Lambert (Ed.), *Bergin and Garfield's handbook of psychotherapy and behavioral change* (pp. 44–83). New York: Wiley.

Slife, B. D., Reber, J. S., & Richardson, F. C. (Eds.). (2005). *Critical thinking about psychology: Hidden assumptions and plausible alternatives*. Washington, DC: American Psychological Association.

Taylor, C. (1997). *Philosophical arguments*. Cambridge, MA: Harvard University Press.

Webster, J. (2013). *The anthropology of protestantism: Faith and crisis among Scottish fishermen*. New York: Palgrave Macmillan.

Zigon, J. (2010). Moral and ethical assemblages. *Anthropological Theory, 10*(1/2), 3–15. doi:10.1177/1463499610370520

Section 2

4 Psychotherapy and the Moral Realism of Charles Taylor

Brent D. Slife, Eric A. Ghelfi, and Nathan M. Slife

There's long been an intriguing tension between the enterprise of psychotherapy and the values of those conducting it. In the early stages of the psychotherapy movement, the goal was to eliminate therapist values altogether, especially personal ones. "Leave your personal values at the therapy room door" seemed to be the maxim of most therapists. The concern was that the power of psychotherapists was so great that *any* values would unduly influence clients and contravene their autonomy to choose their own life path (Deustch & Murphy, 1955; Tjeltveit, 1986; American Psychological Association, 1992). More recently, many researchers and psychotherapists have realized that any such elimination of therapist values is practically impossible (Kelly, 1990; Patterson, 1989; Slife, Smith, & Burchfield, 2003). Therapists cannot help but value their values. For this reason, it is now considered better to acknowledge their presence and take their impact into account than to assume their absence and leave their influence unrecognized (e.g., Slife, Scott, & McDonald, 2016).

The primary issue for therapists at this point is "which values?" If personal and professional values are inescapably involved in therapy, how can we know whether they are the right values? Even the widely held professional value of client autonomy—i.e., the therapist should value the client's preferences above all—is itself a value. In fact, such individual autonomy has often been associated with problematic forms of liberal individualism, which is considered a prime cultural culprit in many client problems (Fowers, Richardson, & Slife, 2017; Chen, Nettles, & Chen, 2009). Indeed, if the client's values are always to hold sway, what happens when those values are somehow part of the client's problem? How then are the right or best values decided? As obviously difficult as these questions are, they are surely at the heart of therapy when therapists inevitably value their values. Yet, they have rarely been considered in therapy research.

The purpose of this chapter is to begin to address this moral "heart of therapy" directly. It does so through the work of Charles Taylor, one of the most revered and thoughtful hermeneutic moral realists of the past six decades (Richardson, Fowers, & Guignon, 1999; Taylor, 1959, 1969, 1979, 1989, 1994c, 2007). If Taylor is right, therapeutic ignorance of the moral ecology of ordinary therapeutic practice is a pivotal ignorance, especially since he believes our core identities and critical approaches to change hinge on them. Indeed, these issues are so important to Taylor that some observers believe his "entire philosophy" and life project is all about practices as the primary source of moral guidance (Brinkmann, 2011, p. 71). And given that therapists and clients both appear—from Taylor's broad definition—to engage in practices, Taylor's hermeneutic approach could conceivably illuminate the moral heart of therapeutic practice itself, including the identity of the professional therapist as well as potential interventions into the identity of the client.

Taylor's Understanding of Morality

To grasp Taylor's approach, we first need to provide some clarification of his understanding of morality. We could probably start with a central claim: "humans are self-interpreting animals" (Taylor, 1985a, p. 4). This claim at least partly implies that humans are self-*evaluators* in the moral sense. Human communities of interpreters constitute the moral meanings of their self-interpretations through their historical traditions and, more importantly for our purposes, their community practices. Taylor believes that if we can articulate these background practices, we can get in touch with the values and goods that animate and define them, which in turn animate and define us as persons.

Practice as Moral Orientation

The notion of practice means more to Taylor than merely engaging in physical activities. He holds that any given practice cannot be meaningful without some orienting sense of the forms of participation and intrinsic standards that are required for competent or excellent performance in the practice (Brinkmann, 2004, 2011; Sugarman, 2006; Taylor, 1989; Yanchar & Slife, in press). Other portions of this book discuss more complex practices (e.g., teaching, publishing, truck driving), and we will later discuss marriage and therapy as practices in this sense. However, let us begin with a deceptively simple practice—riding a bicycle—to reveal some of the rudiments of practice according to Taylor.

Two forms of participation in learning to ride a bike involve maintaining one's balance and avoiding pedestrians. For many people the latter— avoiding pedestrians—will seem more "moral," more like a value, than the former—maintaining balance. However, Taylor views both as part of the "shoulds" and "oughts" of bicycle riding: one *should* maintain balance and one *ought* to avoid pedestrians. Both activities are moral because they matter and have merit in bike riding. Both are also connected to broader senses of morality because losing one's balance and hitting a pedestrian can result in significant harm. In this sense, these activities are orienting reference points for riding a bike that can be said to be intrinsic moral standards, because without them the practice does not exist.

In fact, one of the striking aspects of the moral reference points for any practice is that humans do not invent or construct them. Practices such as bicycle riding require, even demand, the micro-values that serve as reference points to perform the practice. One simply cannot ride a bike without maintaining balance and avoiding pedestrians. These moral requirements are *real* in that they are non-arbitrary and non-subjective, because they are situated in real contexts with real equipment. To be sure, the shoulds and oughts of bike riding can vary to some degree from one context to another, such as professional racing to casual play, but the moral themes of balance and pedestrian avoidance still exist across many cultures and eras. Engaging in these moral themes allows humans as self-interpreting animals to know, at least in part, what matters to those engaged in the practice.

Even so, the ordinary ethic inherent in practices may seem *too* ordinary to really matter. Maintaining bicycle balance, for instance, may seem morally trivial to many readers. Nevertheless, what is viewed as trivial is itself part of the interpretation of the self-interpreter, according to Taylor. From the formalist or deontological ethical tradition, for example, morality is interpreted as a set of philosophical principles derived from formal and deep reflection. If the reader associates this tradition with "morality," then the moral dictum to "maintain one's bicycle balance" will surely seem trite. However, from the perspective of Taylor's hermeneutic tradition, the profound philosophical principles of the deontological tradition might be the more trivial, primarily because they are so thin and abstract that they rarely apply to anything we truly encounter in our practical lives. The more significant values, in Taylor's hermeneutic sense, are the everyday micro-values that allow us to get things done, know how to get better, and clarify who we are in the process.

The Moral Pluralism of Practice

One of the intriguing aspects of personal and particular practices is that there can be so many of them. There are not only different practices, from bike riding to marriage, but also the practices themselves are embedded within different situations and cultures. For these reasons, Taylor believes in a multiplicity of goods. Some may be quite general (perhaps even universal), while others have a more limited collectivity (e.g., specific to a culture), and still others are more particular and unique to a situation (Abbey, 2014; Taylor, 1985b, p. 244). These different goods are not only plural in the quantitative sense but also plural in the qualitative sense. That is, they can involve qualitatively different types that "cannot always be harmoniously combined into principles or reduced to some more ultimate or foundational good" (Abbey, 2014, p. 12). Indeed, some things worthy of affirmation are irreconcilable with others. As Taylor says, "There is no guarantee that universally valid goods should be perfectly combinable, and certainly not in all situations" (Taylor, 1989, p. 61).

This moral pluralism runs counter to the usual Western forms of morality, such as a code of ethics or a set of principles. Taylor's practice emphasis means that we need to unlearn some of our Western habits of understanding, specifically the way we tend to abstract morality from practice, such as formalism and deontology (Slife & Ghelfi, in press). Too often, from Taylor's perspective, people in the West want to emulate the reductionism of the natural sciences and establish laws and principles of morality. As Taylor would see it, this desire is a

> deeply entrenched intellectual habit or outlook characteristic of our kind of society. . . . Single principle explanations work against complex, multi-faceted understandings of human life, but they benefit from association with the tremendous prestige of natural science explanations that . . . seem to reduce complex phenomena to single principles and laws.
>
> (Taylor, 1994c, p. 177)

However, he believes that the world is too diverse and complex to be abstracted or categorized in this manner.

Still, if Taylor is right and we take seriously the plurality of moral practices, we return to the problem at the outset of this chapter: which values are better? What happens when moral values conflict? Taylor realizes that the most dominant approach to this plurality in Western culture is to assume that these questions cannot really be addressed at all, that no values or moral frameworks are better than any other values or frameworks—relativism. Relativism presumes that all individual preferences and cultural values are fundamentally equivalent in their goodness and that moral distinctions are more apparent rather than real (see Introduction). Taylor explicitly rejects this dominant understanding. Indeed, to assume the ultimate equality of moral frameworks is to deny morality altogether, because the purpose of morality is to distinguish what has worth or merit, what is good over what is not as good.

Strong Evaluation

How then does Taylor recognize the plurality of morality and yet answer the moral realist question of which values are better? His answer partly concerns our ability to evaluate the goods of our lives, what he calls "strong evaluation." This term captures Taylor's belief that individuals rank some of their desires, or the goods that they desire, as qualitatively higher or worthier than others. Our capacity for strong evaluations harkens back to the human capacity for self-interpretation (Taylor, 1985a, p. 4), because these interpretations are moral in nature: "the qualitative distinctions we make between different actions, or feelings, or modes of life, as being in some way morally higher or lower, noble or base, admirable or contemptible . . . are central to our moral thinking and ineradicable from it" (Taylor, 1985b, p. 234).

To understand what strong evaluation is, it might be helpful to know what it isn't. In keeping with its non-abstractive nature, this moral capacity isn't necessarily a philosophical reflection on a practice or on morality itself. As Taylor puts it,

> I don't consider it a condition of acting out of a strong evaluation that one has articulated and critically reflected on one's framework. . . . I mean simply that one is operating with a sense that some desires, goals, aspirations are qualitatively higher than others.
>
> (Taylor, 1994b, p. 249)

Nor is strong evaluation a moral principle in the formalist or deontological tradition, such as "follow your strong evaluations." Not only can strong evaluations conflict for an individual; an individual may not act in accordance with the objects of their strong evaluation (Taylor, 1989, p. 62). If anything, Taylor believes that the abstractive tradition of the West has partly led to this moral conflict (Taylor, 1989, pp. 84, 90). This tradition has emphasized the abstraction of morality and thus tended to suppress the role of qualitative distinctions in practical-moral living (Slife & Ghelfi, in press).

Strong evaluations are also not relativistic or subjectivistic. Unlike relativism, Taylor believes that values and moral frameworks *can* distinguish worth and merit. He specifically denies, for example, the claim of relativist Jean Paul Sartre that we are fundamentally clueless about moral choices because we ultimately have no criteria or priorities to direct these decisions (Taylor, 1985a, pp. 29–33). As we will see in applying strong evaluation to therapy, Taylor describes intriguing ways of distinguishing which rival goods are better. Similarly, morality is not merely subjective, relegated to individual preferences and desires: "I want to speak of strong evaluation when the goods putatively identified are not seen as constituted as good by the fact that we desire them, but rather are seen as normative for desire" (Taylor, 1985b, p. 120). In this sense, he views strong evaluations as grounded in the morally real: "Strongly valued goods command the respect of individuals because of their intrinsic value; they are experienced as making calls or demands upon individuals, rather than being freely or arbitrarily chosen by them" (Taylor, 1989, pp. 4, 20). As we engage our therapy example, we will see how Taylor recurs to "human constants" that belie mere subjectivity and ground the intrinsic value of strongly valued goods.

Marital Therapy as Moral Practice

Can Taylor's moral approach to practice inform psychotherapy practice, specifically marital therapy? First, there's no question that he would consider marriage a practice with moral reference points. He would readily acknowledge that this practice is influenced greatly by individual preferences, historical developments, and cultural values, which are themselves part of the moral reference points. However, even with these differences across marriages, there are important moral shoulds and oughts involved in many if not all of these specific practices, such as prioritizing the marital partner or desiring a quality relationship, however these practices are contextually expressed.

In fact, it is the recognition of these *particular* contextual factors that allow the ordinary ethic of marriage to be more clearly specified. Put another way, the contextual particulars of each marital situation can help us to understand even better the logic of the particular moral reference points involved. In the context of American marriages, for example, marital practice typically implies signs of affection (e.g., a touch, a kiss, a service) as well as personal recognition between partners at times of greetings and partings (e.g., a gesture, "I love you"). In this sense, a particular configuration of contextual factors, such as being American, can allow greater knowledge of the moral logic of the relationship, including what a good or bad marriage means within the culture.

How would a marital therapist informed by Taylor's understanding of practical morality go about helping a bad marriage to become better? Taylor would seem to suggest at least two moral moves: articulation of the moral background and consideration of the good that is better.

Articulation

Articulation helps people to become aware of and to understand the practice values of which they are unaware. Articulation is a self-interpretation of sorts, because it foregrounds many of the strongly held values and moral frameworks that people live by and remain in the background of their awareness.[1] It is typically only in times of conflict or crisis that we spell out and defend the assumptions and presuppositions that underlie our moral values and practices (Taylor, 1989, p. 9). Because of the latent quality of underlying sources of moral values, practices, and attitudes, an important role of moral theory and perhaps even good psychotherapy for Taylor is articulation, bringing into awareness certain facets of that which is unspoken but presupposed (Abbey, 2014, p. 41).

For this reason, Taylor would contend that these "latent" micro-values or ordinary ethics drive the practices of problem marriages. In other words, whether good or bad marriages, all are practices underlaid with orienting moral reference points that lead marital partners to treat one another the way they do. Indeed, from a therapeutic perspective, marital partners can even be "congratulated" and perhaps even praised in marital therapy (a type of therapeutic "positive reframing") for their morality, because they are never without some type of values. Both partners may even be said to care about the other partner and the marriage itself, no matter how misguided their values may be. The central issue, then, is what these values are and whether they appropriately serve the practice of a particular marriage.

The partners may, of course, have conscious knowledge of some of their values, but Taylor's contention is that there are often, if not always, core background values that both partners have not labeled or conceptualized. These unconscious values are obviously difficult to change until they are identified and put into question. Generally, articulating this tacit background of moral life requires eliciting the ideals that draw people to a particular moral outlook and inspiring them to act in accord with it. More particularly, Taylor describes six related functions of articulation that may facilitate this process in therapy (Abbey, 2014, pp. 40–47). We only have space for a brief explanation of each here, but we follow these explanations with a therapy case for illustration:

1. Deepen understanding by showing what underpins moral values and actions; "to articulate a framework is to explicate what makes sense of our moral responses" (Taylor, 1989, p. 26).
2. Heighten awareness of the complexity (and messiness) of moral goods; Taylor hopes that understanding the plurality of goods will reduce the appeal of theories that artificially harmonize different goods (Taylor, 1989, p. 107).
3. Awareness increases the chances of rational examination; "conflicts by themselves don't refute. But this doesn't mean that they are unarbitratible, or insurmountable" (Taylor, 1994a, p. 204).

4. Articulation provides a corrective to "the [self-] enforced inarticulacy" of much modern moral philosophy; Taylor argues that these theories are not helpful for fostering the qualitative discriminations that are necessary to moral life (Taylor, 1995, p. 153).

5. Some revealed values are problems, but others need to be reinvigorated; "a moral source is something that when turned toward and articulated can empower one to act in a way prescribed by the full moral view" (Taylor, 1994c, p. 184).

6. After identifying the good that originally inspired the marital partners, they can appreciate how their marital practices have distorted this vision or other possibilities they could nourish; "retrieving [moral sources] might allow us to recover some balance" (Taylor, 1991, p. 96).

Marital Therapy Case

As part of a marital therapy case, George[2] could not understand why he so easily "goes off" verbally on his wife, frequently alienating her (quotes from George). George, in this sense, could not understand his own motives, which for Taylor ultimately involve the moral reference points of his practice of marriage. To articulate these reference points, the therapist attempted to "deepen understanding" of his hidden values, specifically through the question of "what makes moral sense of [your] actions" (articulation function 1 from preceding list). Through the ensuing discussion, George realized that he dealt with his wife "very aggressively" as if an aggressive response was necessary to "win the moral high ground." This understanding helped him to realize the familiarity of this moral position in another context, that of his law practice. "Too frequently," he felt he had to respond aggressively to other lawyers to win the moral high ground in legal cases.

This consistency between his law practice and his marital practice helped him to pinpoint another important moral reference point he'd long held but never put into words: "moral integrity involves complete consistency." George had long assumed that his integrity required similar actions regardless of the difference in circumstances. To treat people differently when the "moral high ground" was at stake was to be "fake" or have a "double standard." Consequently, he treated his wife like he treated opposing attorneys. However, and in line with 2 (preceding list), the therapist asked whether he should consider that different contexts might allow different values, something that George, a religious man, had to consider carefully (3). With some facilitation from the therapist, George explored the possibility that he was misinterpreting some religious precepts (4). As a result, he relented on the "consistency" of his moral integrity in the favor of "making an exception" regarding his "sweet wife." He believed his religion held that love trumped even the possibility of a "double standard" in this regard (5). George subsequently not only acted less aggressively toward her in marital arguments but also "let her win most of the time," leading to a "much happier home life" (6).

Deciding the Better

At this point, we could certainly argue that George's interaction with the therapist helped to change his moral reference points. However, we could also understand this interaction as the therapist using "immanent critique" to resolve George's marital problems (Brinkmann, 2011, p. 70). Immanent critique, in this case, would mean that George realized through therapy a conflict in his *own* moral reference points and opted through moral examination for a moral reference point that he strongly evaluated as higher, his love for his wife. George did not so much *change* his values as become more *consonant* with them. The therapist, in this sense, helped him to "critique" his own "immanent" moral logic or ordinary marital ethic.

From this perspective, the case of George does not necessarily differentiate moral realism from moral anti-realism, because there is nothing in the case that evidences the reality of George's morality. George, for instance, could have been viewed as ultimately acting in consonance with his personal preferences (his love values over his consistency values), which do not have to be considered any more *real* or any more moral than anyone else's preferences. In fact, his preferences could be considered merely subjective or even arbitrary in nature.

A more important test of Taylor's moral realism is a therapeutic situation in which the therapist believes the client's *own* perceived values need to change in better alignment with the real and non-subjective values of the client's practices. Although, as we will see, this situation is more prevalent in the practice of therapy than typically realized, the moral foundations of modern psychology have no resources for dealing with it. Therapists are ethically prohibited from "imposing" their values on clients, and the client is considered to have ultimate autonomy, disallowing the therapist from countermanding the client's values and goals (American Psychological Association, 2010). How, then, might Taylor's moral realist approach provide resources for addressing this ethical dilemma? Here, Taylor actually points to two aspects of deciding the good, contextual comparison and human constants.

First, good values are those that enrich our practices by enabling us to lead *better* lives. We italicize "better" here because Taylor does not believe that a truly situated or contextual understanding of the moral, from the hermeneutic perspective, can provide any kind of complete or final understanding—a "best" for all time. It can only provide a moral superiority to its rival, not a superiority across all cultures or eras. As Schwandt (2000) put it, "For Taylor, what counts as better interpretation is understood as justified movement from one interpretation to another" (p. 202). Still, the issue is what *justifies* this movement when comparing one moral context to another. Here Taylor points to what Nicholas Smith (2002) calls "epistemic gain:" "as one interpretation makes more sense of the phenomenon than a rival one, by resolving contradictions in the rival interpretation, for instance, or by bringing otherwise hidden aspects more clearly into view" (p. 125). This approach to justification could perhaps account for the case of George. Hidden aspects of his religion came "into view," allowing him to move away from one set of reference points to another.

The second aspect that Taylor believes is often needed to decide good interpretations are "human constants" (Taylor, 1981, p. 205; cf. Smith, 2002, p. 125). Although he is exquisitely sensitive to the diversity of moral values among individuals and across cultures, Taylor believes some goods are common to all moral codes and strongly valued by all cultures.[3] These constants revolve around the idea of the value of human life and the dignity of the person: "Every moral system has a conception of what we might call human dignity, . . . of the quality which, in man, compels us to treat him with respect, or . . . a conception which defines what it is to have respect for human beings" (Taylor, 1986, p. 53). In this sense, the case of George could be seen as involving a constant of humanity. After George realized and articulated the background reference points that led to his unproductive fights with his wife, he opted instead for the dignity and respect of his marital partner, something that he experienced as having intrinsic value.

Even so, Taylor does not mean that this "intrinsic value" or its relation to human constants is somehow independent of George's practices. Formalist principles are often abstracted from practices through philosophical reflection and considered good in themselves, separable from humans. Taylor's human constants, on the other hand, are the constants of humans, and thus are human-dependent generalities, by definition (Taylor, 1989, p. 59). They stem from the good that human beings experience, which command their respect in a non-anthropocentric way, as neither deriving solely from human will nor depending only on the fact of individual affirmation (Taylor, 1989).[4]

Other Therapy Applications

Now that we understand some of the tools that Taylor believes are available to the hermeneutic moral realist, such as contextual comparisons and human constants, let us return to the therapeutic dilemma posed at the outset of this section—the therapist's conviction that a client's values are wrong for him or her. We should first note that this dilemma is not really as rare in therapy as it might first seem, though it's rarely made this explicit. In fact, it is tempting to say on Taylor's behalf that therapists are likely not only to routinely discuss values with clients but also to frequently urge clients to modify their values (Fowers, 2005; Slife et al., 2016).

As a prominent case in point, consider the suicidal client. To be suicidal, by definition, means that clients affirm the value of killing themselves. Clearly, some therapists would protest this moral characterization, contending that many suicidal people are merely "irrational," and thus "not thinking clearly" as they move toward suicide. Taylor, however, would undoubtedly note that this valuing of rationality, especially this particular view of rationality, is itself a hidden therapist value. To override a client's clear desire to kill oneself because the therapist has decided that this desire is "irrational" is still to deny the client's autonomy over their own desires and values. And what if the client wishes to be "irrational" in a non-lethal sense, say, at a party—to have fun? Few therapists would object to this irrationality. No, the real reason that therapists resist a client's desire to commit suicide, Taylor would likely suggest, is its clear connection to the dignity and value of life—the human constants that can ground strong evaluations. Indeed, as a testament to these constants, this evaluation is so strong that therapists apparently value them more than the pervasive professional value of protecting client autonomy.

Still another example of therapists fairly routinely aspiring to change a client's values might illustrate Taylor's approach to comparison. Consider how empirical research has shown that "open-minded" therapists—presumably those who are *especially* open to the client's values—do not accept the values of "closed-minded" clients (e.g., Slife et al., 2003). These therapists, instead, attempt to influence their closed-minded clients to become more open-minded like them, in clear violation of the professional value of client autonomy as well as important disciplinary ethical principles that disallow the imposition of therapist values (American Psychological Association, 2010). What is going on here, especially when such therapists are rarely, if ever, brought up on ethics charges? Similar to the issue of suicide, there appears to be an implicit disciplinary understanding that such ethical violations are somehow appropriate. Yet in this case, the therapist's attempt to "convert" the client to open-mindedness is not as clearly related to human constants.

As several observers of psychotherapy have noted (Richardson et al., 1999; Slife, 2008; Slife et al., 2016), there are pervasive professional and cultural values that lead therapists to assume that closed-mindedness cannot possibly be the right value for a client's life. Here, the therapist becomes aware of and provides labels for a potential comparison of two or more client practices—what Taylor would consider a "language of perspicuous contrast," which then allows the client to "formulate both their way of life and ours as alternative possibilities . . ." (Taylor, 1981, p. 205). One could certainly question whether therapists *should* attempt to change their clients' closed-mindedness, but the issue here is how easily the therapist justifies the change in the client's values, in spite of significant ethical principles to the contrary.

We believe in this case that Taylor would point to practices within the professional community, which contain within them background moral reference points that therapists only dimly recognize, if at all. Indeed, it is because these values are relatively unrecognized that they may be so automatically deployed. In any case, the "open-minded" therapist is yet another example of the therapeutic need to change client values. The clear advantage of Taylor's hermeneutic moral realism is that therapists, and perhaps their clients too, understand not only *that* they are doing so but also *what* moral reference points are involved.

Conclusion

This application of Taylor's moral philosophy to psychotherapy may seem an improbable one. Yet, it is easy to see how Taylor might appreciate this kind of implementation, not to mention the moral resources this application might provide the field of psychotherapy. He does not seem to comment directly on psychotherapy in this regard, but many of his writings would certainly support its use. In fact, Taylor's concerns with human identity and change are similar in many ways to the concerns of practicing therapists. He just frames them in terms of the practices and ordinary ethics that many conventional approaches to psychotherapy have backgrounded.

With respect to identity, Taylor believes background practices reveal the core identities of the people who inhabit them, whether they are professional practices (e.g., therapy, business) or personal practices (e.g., marriage, friendship). Indeed, he declares explicitly that "your identity is therefore defined by certain evaluations which are inseparable from ourselves as agents. Shorn of these we would cease to be ourselves" (Taylor, 1985a, p. 34). Values and goods provide important yardsticks of personal success or failure, development or decline. Acting in accordance with them brings a sense of pride, satisfaction, and achievement, whereas acting against or ignoring them leaves one with a sense of failure or dejection (Taylor, 1995, p. 142). Are not these goods also the concerns of many psychotherapists?

Clearly also, articulating our background practices provides a vital avenue of change that has been relatively overlooked in our value-averse psychotherapy culture. By becoming more aware of, and then articulating the values laden in these frequently unconscious practices, Taylor argues that we can sometimes modify them, as in the case of George. Indeed, are not many therapists already sensitized to, if not trained in, making the unconscious conscious? Would it be that much of a stretch to uncover the ordinary ethics of vital human practices such as marriage in this manner? The way to do this uncovering is *not* to strip them of their values-oriented "biases" to get to their objective and pristine nature, which is the training of many therapy institutions. Rather, it is to articulate the moral reference points that define and motivate these practices, allowing them to stand in bold relief, so they can be examined and compared, and the good can be discerned in the relation between unique contexts and human constants.

Notes

1. "Our attempts to formulate what we hold important must, like descriptions, strive to be faithful to something. But what they strive to be faithful to is not an independent object with a fixed degree and manner of evidence, but rather a largely inarticulate sense of what is of decisive importance" (as Taylor, 1985a, p. 38).
2. To protect the confidentiality and identity of this client, many incidental aspects of this case have been changed, including his name.
3. Some commentators accuse Taylor of essentialism here (e.g., Bohman, 1991), meaning that Taylor relies on metaphysical assumptions that are "uninterpreted human constants" (p. 133), which would violate his hermeneutic tenets. However, we agree with Smith (2002) that Taylor's human constant is "simply the embeddedness of human beings in the world and their need to cope with it" (p. 134), which means these constants are the constants of human interpreted experience.
4. Until a moral theory emerges that can explain the human urge to consider goods as if they had an independent existence, Taylor believes that moral realism is the most persuasive approach to moral life.

References

Abbey, R. (2014). *Charles Taylor*. New York: Routledge.

American Psychological Association. (1992). *American Psychological Association ethical principles and code of conduct*. Retrieved May 11, 2017, from www.apa. org/ethics/code/index.aspx

American Psychological Association. (2010). *American Psychological Association ethical principles and code of conduct*. Retrieved May 11, 2017, from www.apa. org/ethics/code/index.aspx

Bohman, J. (1991). *New philosophy of social science: Problems of indeterminacy*. Cambridge, MA: MIT Press.

Brinkmann, S. (2004). Psychology as a moral science: Aspects of John Dewey's psychology. *History of the Human Sciences, 17*(1), 1–28.

Brinkmann, S. (2011). *Psychology as a moral science: Perspectives on normativity.* New York: Springer.

Chen, Y., Nettles, M. E., & Chen, S. W. (2009). Rethinking dependent personality disorder: Comparing different human relatedness in cultural contexts. *The Journal of Nervous and Mental Disease, 197*(11), 793–800.

Deustch, F., & Murphy, W. F. (1955). *The clinical interview.* New York: International Universities Press.

Fowers, B. J. (2005). *Virtue and psychology: Pursuing excellence in ordinary practices.* Washington, DC: American Psychological Association.

Fowers, B. J., Richardson, F., & Slife, B. (2017). *Frailty, suffering, and vice: Flourishing in the face of human limitations.* Washington, DC: American Psychological Association.

Kelly, T. (1990). The role of values in psychotherapy: A critical review of process and outcome effects. *Clinical Psychology Review, 10,* 171–186.

Patterson, C. H. (1989). Values in counseling and psychotherapy. *Counseling and Values, 33,* 164–176.

Richardson, F. C., Fowers, B. J., & Guignon, C. B. (1999). *Re-envisioning psychology: Moral dimensions of theory and practice.* San Francisco, CA: Jossey-Bass.

Schwandt, T. (2000). Three epistemological stances for qualitative inquiry: Interpretivism, hermeneutics, and social constructionism. In N. Denzen & Y. Lincoln (Eds.), *Handbook of qualitative research.* London, UK: Sage Publications.

Slife, B. D. (2008). A primer of the values implicit in counseling research. *Counseling and Values, 53*(1), 8–21.

Slife, B. D., & Ghelfi, E. (in press). A new wave of thinking in psychology. In T. Teo (Ed.), *Contemporary challenges of theoretical psychology: Re-envisioning theoretical psychology and its relations to psychology.* New York: Palgrave Publications.

Slife, B. D., Scott, L., & McDonald, A. (2016). The clash of liberal individualism and theism in psychotherapy: A case illustration. *Open Theology, 2*(1), 595–604.

Slife, B. D., Smith, A. M., & Burchfield, C. (2003). Psychotherapists as crypto-missionaries: An exemplar on the crossroads of history, theory, and philosophy. In D. B. Hill & M. J. Kral (Eds.), *About psychology: Essays at the crossroads of history, theory, and philosophy* (pp. 55–72). Albany, NY: State University of New York Press.

Smith, N. H. (2002). *Charles Taylor: Meaning, morals, and modernity.* Cambridge, UK: Polity Press.

Sugarman, J. (2006). John Macmurray's philosophy of the personal and the irreducibility of psychological persons. *Journal of Theoretical and Philosophical Psychology, 26*(1–2), 172–188. doi:10.1037/h0091273

Taylor, C. (1959). Ontology. *Philosophy, 34,* 125–141.

Taylor, C. (1969). Two issues about materialism: Review of a materialist theory of mind by D. M. Armstrong. *Philosophical Quarterly, 19,* 73–79.

Taylor, C. (1979). *Hegel and modern society.* Cambridge, MA: Cambridge University Press.

Taylor, C. (1981). Understanding and explanation in the geisteswissenschaften. In S. Holtzman & C. Leich (Eds.), *In Wittgenstein: To follow a rule* (pp. 191–210). London, UK: Routledge.

Taylor, C. (1985a). *Philosophical papers I: Human agency and language.* Cambridge, MA: Cambridge University Press.

Taylor, C. (1985b). *Philosophical papers II: Philosophy and the human sciences.* Cambridge, MA: Cambridge University Press.

Taylor, C. (1986). Human rights: The legal culture. In P. Ricoeur (Ed.), *Philosophical foundations of human rights* (pp. 49–57). Paris: UNESCO Publications.

Taylor, C. (1989). *Sources of the self: The making of the modern identity.* Cambridge, MA: Harvard University Press.

Taylor, C. (1991). *The malaise of modernity.* Ontario: Concord. Reprinted 1992 as *The ethics of authenticity.* Cambridge, MA: Harvard University Press.

Taylor, C. (1994a). Précis & reply to commentators in symposium on sources of the self. *Philosophy and Phenomenological Research, 54*(1), 185–186, 203–213.

Taylor, C. (1994b). Reply and rearticulation. In J. Tully & D. Weinstock (Eds.), *Philosophy in an age of pluralism: The philosophy of Charles Taylor in question* (pp. 213–257). Cambridge, MA: Cambridge University Press.

Taylor, C. (1994c). Philosophical reflections on caring practices. In S. B. Phillips & P. Benner (Eds.), *The crisis of care* (pp. 174–187). Washington, DC: Georgetown University Press.

Taylor, C. (1995). A most peculiar institution. In J. E. J. Altham & R. Harrison (Eds.), *World, mind and ethics: Essays on the ethical philosophy of Bernard Williams* (pp. 132–155). Cambridge, MA: Cambridge University Press.

Taylor, C. (2007). *A secular age.* Cambridge, MA: Harvard University Press.

Tjeltveit, A. C. (1986). The ethics of value conversion in psychotherapy: Appropriate and inappropriate therapist influence on client values. *Clinical Psychology Review, 6*(6), 515–537.

5   The Moral Affordances of Publishing Practices

Joshua W. Clegg

One of the implications of the hermeneutic moral realist position outlined in the first part of this book is that all scientific practices are embedded in a moral ecology; that is, they entail and enact stances toward the good and are thus "justified" within a moral framework. Scientific justification has been most often understood as either a rationalist appeal to logical consistency or an empiricist appeal to "data," but hermeneutic moral realism points us toward justification as a moral practice. Understood in this way, justification is not fundamentally about warranting a claim logically or empirically, but about making just (right, true, virtuous, proper, correct, etc.) the historical practices through which understanding is pursued and expressed. Justification of this sort entails a careful attention to the moral affordances of any given practice; an attempt to understand the moral questions and dilemmas raised by that practice and to meet the moral demands it inscribes.

In this chapter, I provide a concrete example of this sort of attentiveness to, in this case, the moral affordances of academic (and, particularly, research) publication practices. Because moral affordances inhere within particular situations and relationships, these are non-abstractable and can only be understood and met in the full concreteness of practice. The following analysis is thus not meant as a definitive statement or demonstration of universalized moral or ethical principles, but as a detailed example of moral attention to a particular context.

At first blush, publication may seem like a mostly technical and auxiliary aspect of scientific justification (i.e., just a medium through which we communicate the actual work of science), and this is partly why I choose to focus on it. When we look closely at any part of the social machinery of science, even something as seemingly bureaucratic as publication, we will see a pervasive fabric of moral choices that fundamentally shapes what we take to be true.

In what follows, I consider the publication process in terms of five areas of concern: collaboration and credit; style and representation; venue, availability, and audience; submission, editorial, and revision; and dissemination and use. In each of the sections corresponding to these concerns, I discuss some of the moral choices and dilemmas, the interpersonal relations and obligations, and the institutional challenges inherent to them. In so doing, I suggest some ways to nurture good faith, equity, and care within these networks of responsibility. I choose to focus on good faith, equity, and care, not because these are the only or ultimate relevant values, but because they seem to me to be the most basic foundation for good, just, virtuous publication practices—that is, when I try to discern right ways to act within the concrete contexts of publication, these are the values that seem to point the way. It is not necessary that you agree with me on that point, but I hope it will become clear that understanding and approaching knowledge practices (including publication practices) in these moral terms is the right thing to do.

Collaboration and Credit

All published texts rely, to some extent, on the labor of others. Thus when I produce a text, I bear responsibility for the labor, collaboration, compensation, and attribution practices involved. I must make decisions about who will bear the costs of this work, who will receive any rewards or credit, and whether these will be distributed fairly, honestly, and with attention to the needs and values of others.

Unfortunately, text production practices often obscure the distributed and stratified community involved in the production of texts. It is not unusual, for example, for parts of a text to be produced by students or clerical staff (e.g., an index or reference list) and this labor is not always credited or compensated. Proofreading, feedback, formatting, research, and other forms of help are also often invisible when a final text is produced. Authorship is one of the primary sources of professional credit, prestige, and influence and is correspondingly carefully guarded in most academic publishing (Biagioli & Galison, 2014). Credit may be distributed in other ways (acknowledgments, footnotes, citations, etc.) but not generally ones that involve holding or granting copyright.

Obviously, it is not always necessary or beneficial to frame collaboration and help in economic terms; sometimes help is a matter of collegiality and reciprocity. But there are other situations where the patina of collegiality can obscure something more like exploitation. Any time that help occurs in relations of unequal power—for example, between professors and students or clerical staff—there is the potential for inequity to be normalized and hidden. Students, for example, often feel (and professors rely on) an obligation to contribute labor with little or no compensation (Freeman, 2000). Sometimes this expectation is made explicit, usually justified in terms of the professional experience students can gain or perhaps in terms of a promised positive letter of recommendation at some time in the future. These dynamics generally rely on a sense of scarce resources—there are limited spots in the best labs or best graduate programs, and students buy entrance and success with their willingness to work for free.

Such exploitative dynamics are neither new nor unique to academic publishing, but are continuous with an apprenticeship tradition that conditions professional access on an indefinite period of obscure and uncredited toil (i.e., "paying your dues") (Dohrer, 1995). Moreover, given the realities of austerity in the contemporary academy (Clawson, 2009), the ineffable rewards of "experience" may be all that are reliably available in most cases. Many students, lab technicians, and clerical staff, however, are often in difficult or precarious financial, legal, or social circumstances, and so their ability to seek fair treatment is severely compromised. For example, a student may need credits from a lab course to keep financial aid that he can't stay in school without; a non-citizen member of the department staff may need her job to keep her worker status; a lab technician may require good performance evaluations to meet the conditions of his parole. These, and many other lesser forms of pressure, can create invisible inequities, constrain choice, or hide coercion under collegiality.

Speaking generally, then, the production of texts involves the distribution of costs and compensations (such as they are), and the geography of this distribution is not always manifest, particularly for those in more privileged positions. Some years ago, a student tried to help me see some of this geography and it was startling how much was simply invisible from my relatively secure position. I suggested that his work could benefit from a slower pace, and he reminded me that he wasn't paid a living wage and that his family's well-being depended on a short time to degree; I suggested that he teach less and he noted that his family wouldn't have health insurance if he didn't teach. Another student showed me how minority students in a doctoral program were often not chosen as collaborators or were given work less likely to receive professional credit and how any attempts to seek fairness or compensation were construed as anti-social or distasteful.

Part of the moral labor of producing a "good" text, then, involves attention to these (and other) possible moral dilemmas. For the hermeneutic moral realist, these dilemmas are neither imagined nor matters of personal inclination. Publication practices and the institutional and personal relationships involved in them have a discernible moral shape that raises unavoidable questions and requires certain forms of action to adequately address them. The good faith and good will of collaborators, for example, is necessary for "good" texts and this is really only possible in an environment of fairness, honesty, and transparency. Yet the real texture of this environment is never fully visible from every position within a graded hierarchy. Thus practices that permit or encourage the voicing of concern or dissent and listening, that provide formal redress, and that explicitly seek to find and ameliorate unfairness or harm are necessary for justifiable publication practices.

Of course, many of the possible inequities or harms inscribed in the various institutional contexts where texts are produced are not within the control of the individual academic. I am not directly responsible for the systemic ways that traditionally oppressed groups are subtly coerced or marginalized; I don't administer the work-study programs or hire clerical staff; I don't drive the publish or perish credit system that commoditizes authorship (Gonzales, 2012). But I am a citizen within these institutional states and I bear the citizen's responsibility to act for their just reformation. I could, for example, take on administrative roles in order to better advocate for low-wage staff; or I could refuse to contribute to organizations or journals with punitive or exploitative practices. There are countless opportunities for such civic responsibility, countless ways to act, yet all of these acts are responses to the same set of basic dilemmas and duties inscribed in the social machinery of academic publication.

Style and Representation

How we write is as much shaped by moral commitments as how we collaborate and distribute publishing credit; yet, academic and research texts generally hide the moral and relational dynamics that constitute them (Billig, 2011). When we write, we are never simply conveying information; we are also taking stands, expressing moral commitments. We show some version of ourselves and others when we write and we can do this with more or less honesty, transparency, and good faith. Historians and sociologists of science have often commented on the ways that research reports "sanitize" the ambiguous, political, and interpersonal processes through which they are produced (e.g., Kuhn, 1970; Niaz, 2010). There may be good reasons for this, but there is also the potential for misleading "our future generations of citizens and scientists, by providing an ahistoric account of progress in science in which presuppositions, contradictions, conflicts and controversies have no role to play" (Niaz, 2010, p. 896).

When we write we are also choosing what and whom to include or exclude, to support or condemn, and these choices reflect both personal and ideological commitments. We will cite, quote, and paraphrase in unequal distributions and these are all ways to comment on what is worthy of attention. We will also directly evaluate the work of others (or ignore it). This process can be (and is generally assumed to be) ideological, a contestation of ideas that reflects what we each value. But this process can also be personal; we can ignore or devalue our competitors, our own collaborators (or students), those we dislike, those who we fear or envy, those whose work we object to on moral grounds, etc. These choices can be mostly implicit or they can be active attempts to distort, misrepresent, or suppress. In all cases, these are moral choices, reflecting what we consider important.

Even seemingly simple questions of style reflect moral commitments. Michael Billig (2011) has written extensively about these. For example, he points to the ways that we often reify abstract concepts (e.g., self-concept or attachment), conferring upon them ontological status and agency, while hiding our own agency, history, and relational qualities. One way we do this in psychology (as in other disciplines) is to deploy nominal forms (e.g., to change "feeling angry" into "affect"), and so "freeze dynamic processes into static entities, and . . . conceal the people who are acting as well as those whom their actions affect" (Quigua & Clegg, 2015, p. 473). We also often make use of the passive voice (e.g., "participants were recruited"), thus obscuring who is acting and the idiosyncrasies of how those choices were made, for what reasons, and who was involved. These are not merely stylistic choices; they are choices to obscure the human, social, and moral qualities of the research process and so project a kind of neutral and mechanical façade over the very human process of doing science.

How we choose to write, then, is both a moral judgment and a moral projection of ourselves, our collaborators, our colleagues, and the issues and phenomena we write about. Our decisions about what to include or emphasize, how to frame or phrase, these are part of the moral labor of writing. In science, at least, the primary function of that labor is to "report" and this is only possible if our readers can discern the persons, relationships, and actions we purport to describe. Our writing will be corrosive of trust and understanding if it cannot reveal the work it is supposed to represent. One duty inscribed in writing research reports is thus to write in ways that are faithful to, and reflective of, the particular human contexts we are reporting on. Writing is also almost always a collaboration in some way[1] and so writing is both a relational negotiation and a power relation where subversions, erasures, and other inequities are possible. Keeping faith with our collaborators and maintaining their good will is thus also an essential task in producing "good" texts.

Institutional forces also heavily pre-structure style and representation in texts. Regulations from human subjects reviews, grant agencies, and universities, for example, often constrain how research participants can be written about. Style manuals, in particular, have a tremendous impact on how texts are constructed and thus on the kinds of persons and activities that can be construed within them. Bazerman (1988), for example, has shown how the conventions enforced by the APA Style manual codified a form of reporting modeled on the physical sciences and so created institutional barriers for qualitative and other kinds of reporting. Writing good texts is thus only possible through work, at the disciplinary and institutional levels, to remove barriers to responsible writing.

Venue, Availability, and Audience

When we choose where and how to publish texts, we also take a stand about the publication practices we endorse, about how ideas or information should be represented, and about who the recipients of that knowledge should be. I can, for example, choose to publish in journals without real peer review (Beall, 2016), in journals that artificially inflate impact factors and citation indices, in journals biased towards positive findings or particular methods, with publishers who only sell to libraries at inflated prices, or who lock texts behind steep paywalls, or even that are part of, or partner with, institutions (corporations, universities, medical facilities, etc.) that engage in harmful, deceitful, or unjust practices.

All forms and venues for publication pair with particular audience profiles and so these choices are also moral stands about who should know about or have access to the texts I produce. I can, for example, publish in venues restricted to the handful of Western scholars whose institutions can afford to penetrate the paywall, or I can publish in outlets with wider access (Van Noorden, 2013). Venues also have histories and knowing these is important for positioning our work in traditions we find morally defensible. The legacies of Hans Eysenck and Raymond Cattell, for example, were tarnished (Winston, 1998) by their participation in *Mankind Quarterly*, an explicitly eugenicist outlet.

Making moral choices about how and where I publish, then, is not merely a matter of choosing the "best" journals, or simply those that will accept my publications, or even those that are taken to be the primary (or "default") journals in my area of scholarship. Much more is at stake in these decisions. In science (as in other areas of scholarship), a primary function of publication is the free dissemination of ideas necessary to maintaining community and improving our bodies of knowledge. Unfortunately, the malformations of knowledge production and dissemination created by corporate and legal constraints in the business of publication (and research) are often inimical to the open and honest exchange of ideas (Van Noorden, 2013). The desires for profit and preferment work together to close down free inquiry and maintain privilege, and to ignore these is simply to be complicit in them.

At least one duty inherent to producing good texts, then, is to choose venues that enhance, rather than impede, the honest, open, and fair exchange of ideas. There are many possible ways to discharge this duty. I can, for example, post in institutional repositories, or work within legitimate open source publication models. I can also participate in administration and oversight in order to advocate for more just publication practices, or choose venues, at least in part, on the basis of their publication practices. However I attend to the justice of my publication practices, good texts and good science are not possible without such attention.

Submission, Editorial, and Revision

These concerns about access are further magnified in the editorial process. The submission and peer review process is generally understood as one of the principle gatekeeping practices in science, and scholarship more generally, and so is already an explicitly moral undertaking. Reviewers and editors are supposed to protect their disciplines from spurious, false, or compromised research methods and claims (Crane, 1967). The commitments of all involved to scrupulous honesty and fairness, to rigorous attention to texts, and to good faith, collegial review practices are thus integral to the proper justification of disciplinary knowledge. Unfortunately, all involved can also manipulate, or at least strain, this system of relational commitments. Prestigious or influential authors, for example, can signal their identities in their (even de-identified) texts in the hope of swaying reviewers or editors; authors can attempt to cite editors or editorial board members in their manuscripts or write flattering cover letters as ways of currying favor; authors can also write coercive, abusive or subtly threatening responses to editors or reviewers in an attempt to force acceptance of their work.

Likewise, editors can manipulate or strain this system by signaling to reviewers the kinds of reviews they want or expect or by choosing reviewers that they know will support their own pre-determinations; editors can intentionally, by manipulation of editorial processes, or unintentionally, by ignoring or "fudging" those processes, privilege certain authors, theoretical orientations, gender orientations, ethnicities, or even their own interests; editors can also "game" the system, encouraging or enforcing citation practices that increase impact factors, inflating rejection rates with invited "dummy" submissions, and so on (Weingart, 2005). Reviewers are probably less likely to stray toward such techniques, mostly because there is little or no extrinsic reward for their work. Rather, reviewers are probably most often tempted to strain the system by producing less-than-rigorous reviews, by trying to give whatever review they think the editor wants, or by simply refusing to participate. Thus, like science in general, the entire peer review process is a delicate human system, easily undermined by bad faith or bad will. This will not be news to anyone involved in academic publishing, but, as the integrity of science, psychology, and essentially all scholarship depends on the integrity of this system, moral failures within it are simply catastrophic to knowledge.

Beyond these systemic considerations, the whole peer review process is also a relational one. Not just authors, but editors, reviewers, and publication staff are frail humans, probably overburdened and undercompensated, probably often ambivalent, exhausted, or confused. Authors can often be fragile, seeking professional access and resources certainly, but also approval, validation of their work and capacities, as well as collegiality and respect. Editors and reviewers are no different (except that these are sometimes a little more secure in their positions within a discipline). The peer review process is thus also an opportunity for care, even if that opportunity is not always (or even often) taken. Authors can acknowledge and respect the usually un- or under-compensated efforts of editors and reviewers; editors and reviewers can show collegiality, respect, encouragement, and kindness, even while offering negative critiques or rejecting manuscripts. All involved can pay greater attention and respect to the many invisible hands in editorial and publication offices that make publication possible.[2]

As in the other facets of publication already discussed, those involved in peer review and editorial processes are caught up in complex systems with many dynamics beyond their control. The journal metric industry (e.g., those that construct and arbitrate impact factors, citation indices, etc.), for example, is most often an external imposition that particular editors or authors can do little to control (Weingart, 2005). Likewise, the financial pressures originating in publishing houses push book and journal review processes toward austerity practices like paywalls and the reduction or elimination of author, editor, and reviewer compensation. Austerity, in general, coming from state legislatures and federal governments, as well as through various corporate mechanisms, encourages competition and manipulation of the peer review system. Even if every author, editor, and reviewer were acting always in good faith and with good will, these larger forces would act against a just and correct body of knowledge. Thus to justify our contributions, we also must be active in creating change in these institutional dynamics. We can contribute to new kinds of publishing initiatives, put pressure on traditional publishing bodies in our roles as editors, authors, and reviewers, work toward better public funding and against corrosive austerity practices, and so on.

Dissemination and Use

My responsibility for what I publish does not end with publication, but extends into that indefinite and uncertain period where others may or may not read or deploy my work to some end. At the least, I should expect a handful of journal readers to see my text and perhaps use it as inspiration or justification for further work. It is also (increasingly) possible that journalists will report on my work or ask me to comment on a story related to that work. Policy makers and administrators of various kinds may even use my work to inform, justify, or challenge particular policies.

I thus have a responsibility to shape my collaborations and interactions with those who will disseminate my publications such that, as much as possible, the integrity of the work is maintained. I think we are most comfortable attending to this obligation in relation to colleagues, as there are natural forms for doing so—we can write commentaries or follow-up articles to clarify our positions and correct what we take to be misinterpretations or misuses of our ideas; we can organize symposia to initiate dialogue; we can communicate with colleagues directly. We can (and usually do) choose to employ civility, fairness, and respect in these situations, and this is generally sufficient to safeguard the integrity of our work and the discipline.

Things, however, can be much more complicated beyond our small academic communities. For example, when textbooks or large review articles discuss our work, these will likely do so in simplified and probably at least somewhat distorted ways. Large reviews of findings have a tendency, in particular, to erase subtleties and caveats and to create a false picture of clarity. Reporting, and particularly science reporting, tends to be even more distorting, as reporters (or, more and more commonly, bloggers) oversimplify, over-interpret, and not infrequently completely misrepresent findings (Caulfield, 2004). Most of us will probably not find our work being cited or deployed in political or administrative contexts, but these too are fraught. Certainly, the most well-known historical cases where psychology has informed policy—for example, mass testing associated with immigration (Gelb, 1986), military interrogations (Pope, 2016), etc.—do not inspire confidence in our capacity to ensure the equitable and benevolent application of research.

We don't really have traditions or formalized processes for attending to our work as it leaves the academic provinces. No doubt, most of us have had this experience in some form or other and we probably weren't quite sure what to do. We may not have thought about questions like: who should have access to the knowledge I produce? What power or resources can it mobilize and how can those be equitably distributed? How available should the knowledge be? How should this knowledge be understood by those who read it? What are the right ways for this knowledge to be deployed, applied, represented, and communicated? How could it be (and how is it) misrepresented, abused, or used to harm, deceive, or oppress? How can I prevent or limit such abuses or harms?

Addressing these dilemmas is rarely straightforward, but at the least we can consider them and allow them to frame our interactions. For example, when we field press requests, we can do some research on the publication and reporter, ensuring ourselves that these are responsible, fair, and rigorous. We can also include conditions on how we will be quoted—for example, requiring that caveats or complexities be included with any statements of findings. We can also follow up on reporting or other forms of dissemination to ensure that our standards are met, writing letters, proposing corrections, or publishing clarifications when necessary. If our work is deployed in applied contexts, we can seek to participate to the degree necessary to evaluate the uses to which our work is put. We can attend legislative hearings, visit institutions, engage in dialogue with administrators, and we can provide clarifications or make requests consistent with our own moral sense. We can also try to anticipate ways that our texts may be misappropriated and attempt to mitigate these where possible. For example, we can include in our reports explicit, clear caveats discouraging inappropriate interpretations or applications. We can also strive to write within our warrant, avoiding the over-generalizations, over-extensions, and semantic slippages common to writing in psychology.

Conclusion

In the case of any given text, not every one of the moral considerations treated here will have an appreciable effect on the text or its use, but *in toto* these constitute its socio-historical texture. Put simply, the text *is* the history of moral choices, interpersonal relations, and political-institutional structures that have produced and continue to maintain it as an artifact of culture. For the hermeneutic moral realist, these moral considerations are not merely subjective projections of preference; they are an elucidation of the most essential nature of the text as a living moral tissue, made just and unjust (false and true; virtuous and vicious) in its unfolding enactments. Careful attention to the moral affordances within these enactments, to the very real persons and communities that produce them, and to the equally real and definite, though situationally specific, justifiable moral choices that constitute them, is how good, and thus true, texts are made.

Notes

1. Even solitary monographs need editors.
2. Kate Sheese (2016) points to an interesting example of this attention in Jane Loevinger's work. Loevinger consistently acknowledged those in more invisible roles, for example commenting on the typists' role in the production of the scoring manual for the Family Problems Scale: "actually, the term typist does injustice to the calibre of judgment required to prepare protocols adequately" (pp. 38–39).

References

Bazerman, C. (1988). *Shaping written knowledge: The genre and activity of the experimental article in science* (Vol. 356). Madison: University of Wisconsin Press.

Beall, J. (2016). Predatory journals: Ban predators from the scientific record. *Nature, 534*(7607), 326–326.

Biagioli, M., & Galison, P. (2014). *Scientific authorship: Credit and intellectual property in science.* Abingdon, UK: Routledge.

Billig, M. (2011). Writing social psychology: Fictional things and unpopulated texts. *British Journal of Social Psychology, 50*(1), 4–20.

Caulfield, T. (2004). The commercialisation of medical and scientific reporting. *PLoS Medicine, 1*(3), e38.

Clawson, D. (2009). Tenure and the future of the university. *Science, 324,* 1147–1148.

Crane, D. (1967). The gatekeepers of science: Some factors affecting the selection of articles for scientific journals. *The American Sociologist,* 195–201.

Dohrer, G. (1995). Student teaching by any other name: The impact of metaphor. *Teaching Education, 7*(1), 125–132.

Freeman, A. (2000). The spaces of graduate student labor: The times for a new union. *Antipode, 32*(3), 245–259.

Gelb, S. A. (1986). Henry H. Goddard and the immigrants, 1910–1917: The studies and their social context. *Journal of the History of the Behavioral Sciences, 22*(4), 324–332.

Gonzales, L. D. (2012). Responding to mission creep: Faculty members as cosmo-politan agents. *Higher Education, 64,* 337–353.

Kuhn, T. S. (1970). *The structure of scientific revolutions* (2nd enl. ed.). Chicago: University of Chicago Press.

Niaz, M. (2010). Science curriculum and teacher education: The role of presupposi-tions, contradictions, controversies and speculations vs Kuhn's "normal science". *Teaching and Teacher Education, 26*(4), 891–899. doi:10.1016/j.tate.2009.10.028

Pope, K. S. (2016). The code not taken: The path from guild ethics to torture and our continuing choices. *Canadian Psychology/Psychologie canadienne, 57*(1), 51.

Quigua, F., & Clegg, J. W. (2015). Imagine the feeling: An aesthetic science of psychology. *Integrative Psychological and Behavioral Science, 49*(3), 459–477.

Sheese, K. (2016). *Beyond mixing methods: Jane Loevinger's integrative psychomet-rics as a case for an aesthetic methodological pluralism.* Unpublished manuscript, Psychology Department, The Graduate Center, City University of New York.

Van Noorden, R. (2013). The true cost of science publishing. *Nature, 495*(7442), 426–429.

Weingart, P. (2005). Impact of bibliometrics upon the science system: Inadvertent consequences? *Scientometrics, 62*(1), 117–131.

Winston, A. S. (1998). Science in the service of the far right: Henry E. Garrett, the IAAEE, and the Liberty Lobby. *Journal of Social Issues, 54*(1), 179–210.

6 Politics and Moral Realism

Frank C. Richardson, Robert C. Bishop, and Kathleen L. Slaney

The introduction to this volume (Slife & Yanchar) explains the need, both theoretical and practical, for a robust moral realism grounded in the hermeneutic philosophy of Heidegger (1962), Gadamer (1989), and Taylor (1985, 1989). Slife and Yanchar argue that most of the approaches to making sense of and advancing a moral outlook in modernity, as their proponents understand them, operate within a broadly "dualist" conception of knowing. That is, objective and subjective realms of knowing are quite separable and we can in principle understand one completely without the other. These authors contend that "subjectivist" approaches, such as individualism and postmodernism or social constructionism confine ethical meaning to a strictly subjective sphere, so that in the end "all moral orders are equally arbitrary" (Brinkman, 2011). "Objectivist" approaches, by contrast, such as many types of evolutionary psychology in one way and the modern rationalist tradition of Kant, Kohlberg, and others in another way, ground moral meaning in strictly objective realities or principles.

Slife and Yanchar (this volume) point out that subjectivist approaches to morality ultimately founder in a sea of relativism because they fail to do justice to the seriousness and inescapability of moral judgments in human life. At the same time, objectivist views are confined to a kind of "abstractland" where they remain significantly disconnected from the real-life contexts and everyday meanings of our practical lives. They also claim a kind of finality or certainty in matters of ethical discernment that ignores the finitude and limits of human beings who can at best "see through a glass darkly." The authors go on to sketch what a nondualist form of morality might look like, drawing on ordinary language philosophy, the practice turn in sociology, and hermeneutic philosophy. A nondualist view promises to illuminate our actual experience of morality in shifting cultural and historical contexts while clarifying how we can and often do achieve a solid moral compass in the real, limited world in which we live.

In this chapter, we suggest that there is a serious lack of and need for moral realism in contemporary political debates as well as in more personal realms of living. Deneen (2018, p. 180) describes the current social and political landscape as one of "pervasive discontent, political dysfunction, economic inequality, civic disconnection, and populist rejection." Stale political ideologies do battle while more and more citizens find their debates hollow and uninspiring. The paralyzing polarization of left and right intensifies and no attractive or convincing alternatives are evident. A distressing nondemocratic, authoritarian populism seems on the rise at home and abroad. The oft-quoted lines of W. B. Yeats (1952) poem "The Second Coming" come to mind:

> The best lack all conviction, while the worst
> Are full of passionate intensity.

It seems to us that theoretical psychology, especially the kind of moral realism discussed in this book, can shed valuable light on this situation.

Our "Neoliberal Condition"

The term "neoliberal" is much bandied about nowadays. What Jeff Sugarman (2013) terms our "neoliberal condition" is often cited as the source of much of this dysfunction and discontent. Sugarman (2015), drawing on the work of influential critics over the last 20 years (Brown, 2003; Davies & Bansel, 2007; Foucault, 2008; Harvey, 2005; Rose, 1999; Sennett, 1998, and others), identifies key features of a neoliberal political economy as

> a radically free market in which competition is maximized, free trade achieved through economic deregulation, privatization of public assets, vastly diminished state responsibility over areas of social welfare, the corporatization of human services, and monetary and social policies congenial to corporations and disregardful of the consequences: poverty, rapid depletion of resources, irreparable damage to the biosphere, destruction of cultures, and erosion of liberal democratic institutions.
> (p. 104)

To complicate the situation somewhat, it appears that this growing neoliberal hegemony has *two* main branches. One is the familiar libertarian approach that touts small government, lowering taxes, and reducing government regulation. But another, on the left, the philosopher and feminist theorist Nancy Fraser (2017) terms "progressive neoliberalism," which in

Fraser's words "mixed together truncated ideals of emancipation and lethal forms of financialization." This movement in recent decades in place of

> the New Deal coalition of unionized manufacturing workers, African Americans, and the urban middle classes . . . forged a new alliance of entrepreneurs, suburbanites, new social movements, and youth, all proclaiming their modern, progressive bona fides by embracing diversity, multiculturalism, and women's rights.

It "deregulated the banking system and negotiated the free-trade agreements that accelerated deindustrialization. What fell by the wayside was the Rust Belt—once the stronghold of New Deal social democracy, and now the region that delivered the electoral college to Donald Trump." She adds that "[t]hroughout the years when manufacturing cratered, the country buzzed with talk of 'diversity,' 'empowerment,' and 'non-discrimination.'" Identifying "progress" with meritocracy instead of equality, these terms equated "emancipation" with the rise of a small elite of "talented" women, minorities, and gays in the winner-takes-all corporate hierarchy instead of with the latter's abolition.

So, the tentacles of neoliberalism reach far and wide into today's society and politics. The ascendency of "meritocracy instead of equality" that Fraser identifies may play a key role in this development. Recent articles by Stewart (2018) and Brill (2018) develop this idea. Brill describes how over the last five decades American society has split "into two classes: the protected and the unprotected. The protected overmatched, overran, and paralyzed the government," the work being "done by a generation of smart, hungry strivers who benefitted from one of the most American values of all: meritocracy." Most Americans "with average incomes have been left to fend for themselves, often at jobs where automation, outsourcing, the decline of union protection and . . . obsession with squeezing out every penny of short-term profit have eroded any sense of security."

"Entrepreneurial Selves"

Sugarman (2015) suggests that even though psychologists are "underequipped . . . to speak of sociopolitical and economic matters," we have no choice but to delve into them." Selfhood, action, and aims in living "take their form from the kinds of relations in which human beings are immersed," while "politics—the organized influence and control of others . . . is a constitutive feature of both collective and individual psychological life." As Rose (1999) incisively puts it, such politics "govern the soul." As a result, Martin and McLellan (2013) argue, psychologists distort their subject matter and probably do more harm than good unless they attend closely to these matters. They contend that, "neoliberalism is reformulating personhood, psychological life, moral and ethical responsibility" and even "what it means to have selfhood and identity." Thus, building on the work of Foucault (2008) and Rose (1999), they astutely identify an "enterprise culture" that mandates, almost to the exclusion of any others, "personal attributes" of "initiative, self-reliance, self-mastery, and risk-taking," essentially the "entrepreneurial activity of individuals."

These are not happy developments for human well-being. For example, William Deresiewicz (2014a, 2014b) describes how an increasing number of students at elite colleges are frightened of not being highly successful. This leads to a "violent aversion of risk" and the loss of a passion for ideas. They give little attention to cultivating skills in critical thinking or questioning assumptions, which play no role in the frantic rush for good grades and other markers of success. They are abetted in this by a curriculum that trains them "in the analytic and rhetorical skills that are necessary for success in business and the professions. Everything is technocratic—the development of expertise—and everything is ultimately justified in technocratic terms." Of course, there are exceptions. However, he contends, "beneath the façade of seamless well-adjustment . . . what you find often are toxic levels of fear, anxiety, and depression, of emptiness and aimlessness and isolation" (Deresiewicz, 2014a). He notes that a large-scale survey of college freshmen recently found that self-reports of emotional well-being have fallen to their lowest level in the study's 25-year history.

In a similar vein, Jacob Sugarman (2018) summarizes research that suggests that neoliberal trends including advancing meritocracy in several Western democracies have a significant influence on our "subjectivity" and "how we view ourselves," with deleterious consequences for emotional well-being. There is some indication that they promote greater "perfectionism" along with more "anxiety, depression, eating disorders and suicidal ideation, not to mention an increased dependence on social media."

The distinguished cultural historian Jackson Lears (2015) suggests that Deresiewicz's analysis applies to much of the wider society. In general, he writes,

> Among the educated and professional classes, no one would be caught dead confusing intellectual inquiry with a quest for ultimate meaning, or with the effort to create an 'independent' or 'authentic' selfhood . . . determined to heed its own ethical and aesthetic imperatives, resistant to the claims of fashion, money, and popularity.

He adds, "In an atmosphere dominated by postmodern irony, pop-neuroscience, and the technocratic ethos of neoliberalism, the self is little more than a series of manipulable appearances, fashioned and re-fashioned to meet the marketing needs of the moment." To a great extent, one pursues rewards that by themselves are hollow and transient, namely the credentials, badges of achievement, and prestige dished out by this kind of meritocracy.

What drives this slide into a neoliberal condition? Mark Lilla (2014) astutely notes that the "social liberalization" of recent decades is "meeting less resistance among educated urban elites nearly everywhere" and a "new cultural outlook" is emerging that "treats as axiomatic the primacy of individual self-determination over traditional social ties, indifference in matters of religion and sex, and the *a priori* obligation to tolerate others." As traditional morality and custom fade, ours becomes "a libertarian age by default: whatever ideas or beliefs or feelings muted the demand for individual autonomy in the past have atrophied." We "give individuals maximum freedom in every aspect of their lives," believing or just hoping that "all will be well."

The Failures of Liberalism

In his much-discussed recent book *Why Liberalism Failed*, Patrick Deneen (2018) traces this cultural outlook centered on individual autonomy back to the beginning of modern times. He indicates that classical and Christian premodernity had long understood that the kind of liberty that forestalled tyranny was a "condition of self-rule" achieved through cultivation of virtues or moral excellences such as "temperance, wisdom, moderation, and justice." Such self-rule always involved a "limitation of desire" (pp. 22–23), self-discipline, and giving precedence to the deeper satisfaction or sense of meaningfulness associated with the achievements of character over sheer quantities of worldly success, prestige, or possessions.[1] Such cultivation of character entails finding a sense of lasting purpose and deeper meaning that may withstand a life's disappointments and tragedies. It goes hand in glove with developing social norms and institutional forms that "check the power of leaders" and allow the "expression . . . (to varying degrees) . . . of popular opinion in political rule" (p. 22). So the personal and the political interpenetrate and support one another.

According to Deneen (2018), a "signal hallmark of modernity" was "the rejection of this long-standing view" of self-rule in personal and political realms. The effort to foster virtue was seen as "both paternalistic and ineffectual," as prone to moralistic abuse and the arbitrary exercise of authority, and as powerless to contend with human selfishness, greed, and pride (as Machiavelli forcefully argued). The novel solution proposed was to base politics "upon the reliability of 'the low' rather than aspiration to 'the high'" (p. 24). In this approach, "liberty" is significantly redefined as "liberation of humans from established authority, emancipation from arbitrary culture and tradition, and the expansion of human power and domination over nature" (p. 27). A much more effective curb on incurably base or self-interested human proclivities—and indeed a way of channeling them in the service of greater productivity and accomplishment—can be provided by strictly external constraints, by "the legal prohibitions and sanctions of a centralized political state" (p. 26). Rather than in any sense "withering away," such a strong political state and legal system becomes essential.

This new liberal voluntarist conception of human nature and agency has contributed, along with the persistence of some older ideals and traditions, to a considerable expansion of human rights and human dignity and to the elimination of many superstitious, arbitrary, irrational limits on human powers and creativity—all this work that remains unfinished today. But it never has explained how profoundly self-interested human persons can be motivated to craft law and policy that will effectively contain their inherent drive for power and possessions. Rather, they are likely to use every political and legal means available, as Brill (2018) and Stewart (2018) have documented has occurred with America's "new aristocracy," in order to enhance and preserve their own and their children's privileged economic and social ascendency. In general, over time, this has "corrosive social and civic effects." It "[u]ndermines any appeal to common goods" and "induces a zero-sum mentality" that infects many different spheres of life and thought (Deneen, 2018, p. 29). This approach manages to be at once brutally realistic bordering on cynical about human nature and wildly optimistic, almost utopian, about its material and moral prospects.

Deneen's (2018) penetrating analysis of these failures of modern liberalism, as he defines it, fits well with other critiques of the kind of one-sided, anti-authoritarian individualism or liberal individualism, from Tocqueville (1969) to the present day (Richardson, Fowers, & Guignon, 1999; Sandel, 1996; Selznick, 1992; Sullivan, 1986; Slife, Smith, & Burchfield, 2003; Bellah, Madsen, Sullivan, Swindler, & Tipton, 1985).[2] He suggests, in effect, that most of the various shortcomings that critics have discussed under the rubrics of liberal individualism or neoliberalism derive in large measure from the misleading philosophical anthropology of liberalism he analyzes.[3] This distinctive ethical and political outlook actually "unites individualism and statism" (Deneen, 2018, pp. 43 ff.).[4] In its own unique way it underpins the kind of liberalism that has become the most influential and long-lasting of the three great political ideologies, along with communism and fascism, of modern times (p. 4).

Democratic Populism

What might a democratic politics look like that 1) breaks free of the philosophical anthropology of voluntarist liberal individualism; and yet 2) preserves indispensable modern ideals of respect for the rights, equal worth, and equal dignity of every human person? Could there be such a thing?

Richardson, Bishop, and Garcia-Joslin (2018) suggest that there are four broad political paths open to us at the moment. One is the standard conservative libertarian approach that advocates mainly reducing taxes, especially on the wealthy, and cutting back on government regulations, evidently leading to increased inequality and increasing citizen revolt. Second is what Fraser (2017) called "progressive neoliberalism," which in her words identifies "'progress' with meritocracy instead of equality." Third is what Fraser terms the "reactionary populism" of Donald Trump followers in 2016 and other similar movements across Western democracies recently, which do not appear to represent a coherent, nonauthoritarian pathway to a better future. Fourth, recently a variety of commentators (Chen, 2016; Mills, 2016; Sewall, 2016; Stoller, 2016, Liu & Hanauer, 2011, and others) writing in diverse publications have begun sketching out the idea a genuine *democratic* populism.

The spirit of democratic populism, of self-rule in a modern context, might take a variety of institutional forms. It might involve such things as the breakup up many monopolies and revitalizing market competition; banning price and data discrimination; proscribing many forms of "vertical integration" where corporations or industries buy retailers or services to exclude rivals from the market; rethinking what reasonable profits for shareholders might mean and promoting higher wages for all employees; and doing much to localize banking, retail, and farming. Deneen (2018) writes of the will, requiring "sacrifice and patience," to "take back control over liberalism's forms of bureaucratized government and globalized economy" (pp. xiv–xv) and of "practices fostered in local settings, focused on the creation of new and viable cultures, economics grounded in virtuosity within households, and the creations of civic polis life" (p. 197). A recent blog post by the redoubtable Andrew Sullivan (2017) speaks to this process. He writes,

> [W]hat we're seeing right now, across the developed world, is a bid to retain the meaning of a culture and a way of life in the headwinds of faceless, placeless economics. [Right-wing nationalism] is one response. The answer to it is not globalism, which is as cold as it is remote, but patriotism, that love of country that does not require the loathing of other places or the scapegoating of minorities or a phobia of change, that confident identity that doesn't seek to run away from

the wider world but to engage it, while somehow staying recognizable across the generations.

A number of these thinkers have found fresh guidance from the writings of Christopher Lasch (1995), especially his posthumously published book of essays, *The Revolt of the Elites*. Sewall (2016) summarizes: "Abandoning the left's original intent to protect the common man, Lasch observed, progressives chose instead to pursue diversity, secularism, and cultural revolution. Families, schools, and churches were left behind." Families, schools, and churches surely have often needed remedy and reform, but overlooking the cultivation of substantive justice, character, and the common good hollows out culture and breeds what the theoretical psychologist Philip Cushman (1990) famously termed "empty selves." From a democratic populist perspective, in Matt Stoller's (2016) words, this "revolt of the elites" means that "[f]or most Americans, the institutions that touch their lives are unreachable." However, "citizens must be able to govern themselves through their own community structures . . . sovereign citizens governing sovereign communities [are] the only protection against demagoguery."

It seems profitable to consider some of Lasch's insights through the lens of moral realism or a nondualist morality. Those ideas can illumine how moral realism might play out in the real world of our political struggles at the same time that a hermeneutic moral realism might beneficially clarify and ground a democratic populist perspective and approach.

Hermeneutic Ontology

Moral realism incorporates a view of our social and historical existence that clarifies both our rich possibilities for meaning and our finitude or insurmountable limits qua human. For example, Charles Taylor (2002) argues that, in both everyday life and more formal human science inquiry, "understanding a text or event which comes to us out of our history should be construed, not on the model of the 'scientific' grasp of an object, but rather on the model of speech-partners who come to an understanding" (p. 126). This sort of "coming-to-understanding" typically concerns clarifying and advancing the many kinds of meanings that people truly live by. The end or goal, in Taylor's words, is "being able in some way to function together with the partner" (p. 128). In this process, 1) we harbor self-defining beliefs and values concerning things we care about greatly, in which we have a "deep identity investment," sometimes in "distorted images we cherish of others" (p. 141). At the same time, since our ideals and our images of others and events are always partial or distorted in some way, we 2) need not just to compromise or go along to get along with others, but to *learn from* the past, others, or other cultures. Thus, we *depend* upon them greatly in matters closest to our own hearts, a demanding and often taxing situation that may, at times, entail a deeply personal, sometimes painful "identity cost" (p. 141) as we struggle to rework distorted or inauthentic meanings and values to which we have become attached.

Hermeneutic philosophy is an unreserved moral *realism*. In this view, particular moral convictions or ideals are an indelible part of being human. They always define us and direct our important choices in the ongoing business of living. On the one hand, they are inescapable. We always judge and react to events in terms of some such values or principles. Accordingly, Taylor (1985) argues that human agents do not simply desire particular outcomes or satisfactions in living, which he terms "weak evaluations." Rather they always, even if only tacitly or unconsciously, make higher-order or "strong evaluations" (p. 3). Namely, they evaluate the quality of their desires and motivations in terms of how they fit in with their overall sense of a good life or decent society. On the other hand, we are limited and imperfect beings. As a matter of integrity, novel circumstances or challenges from others with different perspectives are bound to provoke continuing rethinking and dialogue on our part. Thus our condition is one that Mikhail Bakhtin (1981) aptly termed "unfinalizability."

In the hermeneutic view, our important meanings and values cannot be altered or revised arbitrarily or for purposes of mere convenience or personal advantage without being subject to judgments of hypocrisy or inauthenticity. Postmodern or social constructionist thinkers might reply that they, too, regard some meanings and values as inescapable or nonarbitrary because of our embeddedness in a particular historical culture. Thus, we have to take them into account in directing or revising our living. However, since such thinkers regard these values as merely constructed for one purpose or another and ultimately strictly relative; they can only construe any reevaluation of them as either 1) a matter of one's "capacity to invite, compel, stimulate, or delight" another and "not on criteria of veracity" (Gergen, 1985, p. 272); or 2) in terms of their "pragmatic implications," the consequences or results they happen to bring about, which are strictly a matter of personal preference (Rorty, 1982).

Moral realism contends that such views clash severely with what we really mean when we invoke important meanings and values in everyday life. Richardson et al. (1999, p. 193) comment:

> One wonders if constructionist thinkers have really thought through what it would mean to collapse the distinction entirely between feeling guilty merely from the fear of disapproval (an unpleasant consequence) versus feeling remorse from violating one's personal moral

standards. Taken literally, that would mean adopting an inhuman and quite destructive amorality.

In any case, postmodern thinkers (to their credit!) typically do not live up to their own beliefs (Richardson et al., 1999, pp. 192–195). They seem to adopt relativism as a humane perspective they feel will help undermine irrational guilt and dogmatic values. They clearly embrace an ideal of human freedom from such influences. Much like liberal individualists, they are embroiled in the contradiction of treating *all* moral values as merely relative or subjective in order to promote *particular* moral values, namely liberty and social peace as they envision them, which they do *not* count as purely relative or optional. By contrast, moral realism obviates such contradictions. In this view, in everyday human experience we encounter moral realities *not* wholly dependent upon our constructions. We struggle to make sense of and appreciate such realities at the same time that they challenge and, if you will, "interpret" us.

The Ideal of Progress

Turning to Lasch, in perhaps his weightiest treatise, *The True and Only Heaven: Progress and its Critics*, published in 1991, Lasch provides a historical and critical study of the doctrine or cult of progress, dominant in American political thought and ideology from the early years of the country to the present. Susan McWilliams (2016) summarizes the idea of progress Lasch critiques as "the faith that we humans can continually improve our lot and standards of living" and that "we should seek to satisfy all our increasing desires" with as little consideration as possible of "natural limits or moral restraints" (p. 12).

In the view of most premodern, classical moral philosophy, of course, this attitude is a recipe for disaster. The achievement of character, inner harmony, or spiritual peace requires placing definite *limits* on the satisfaction of mere desires, which multiply endlessly even though they fail in the end to really satisfy. For Plato, the realm of desire by itself is a kind of "chaos." That all changes in modern times, beginning with Descartes (Taylor, 1989, pp. 143 ff.), who saw no problem with the proliferation of desires so long as it was possible to gain steady *instrumental* control over the business of satisfying them. In that case, the more the merrier.

This notion of progress can be traced back to the eighteenth-century founders of modern liberalism (Hobbes, Locke, etc.) who argued that "because human beings are creatures of insatiable desire, there needed to be a continual increase in productive capacities to satisfy those desires" (McWilliams, 2016, p. 14). Lasch (1991) contends that today both the political left and political right *share* the same deep "belief in the desirability and inevitability of technical and economic development" (p. 23). For those on the left, this kind of exaggerated "technological optimism" is coupled with "cultural cosmopolitanism" and "various doctrines of personal liberation" while those on the right add to the mix a "program of market deregulation" and an unqualified "vision of unending economic growth" (McWilliams, 2016, pp. 12–13).

In Lasch's (1991, p. 23) view, the problem with this one-sided doctrine of unending progress is that it is "self-defeating." It leads to or at least contributes substantially to such evils and dilemmas as a widening gap between rich and poor nations, flagrant inequality at home, insurrections and terrorism against the West, collapse of the middle class, self-serving elites at the top of both political parties in the US, authoritarian populist movements in ostensible Western democracies, deterioration of the planet's climate and resources, and pervasive cultural and moral degradation in what Chen (2016) calls "a society focused on meritocratic, materialistic success."[5]

In *The True and Only Heaven*, Lasch chronicles the fascinating history of neglected or forgotten thinkers from the American revolution into the twentieth century, like Randolph Bourne, Orestes Brownson, Josiah Royce, and Georges Sorel, who along with others like Jonathan Edwards and Ralph Waldo Emerson, keenly detected many of the flaws of "progress" and a hurtling capitalism. They had very little success in envisioning clear or plausible alternatives. But they comprise a somewhat coherent anti-progressive "populist" tradition of thought, with which Lasch feels we need to reconnect. He felt it might be possible to embrace such populism without nativism and anti-intellectualism. Some of its ideals and qualities might include more in the way of small-scale production and political decentralization, resistance to innovation for innovation's sake, endorsement of a petty bourgeois stress on loyalty, hard work, and self-discipline, actively self-governing communities as opposed to rule by technocratic experts, and the "pursuit of useful callings (as opposed to luxury and worldly success)" (McWilliams, 2016, p. 14).

The Revolt of the Elites

In *The Revolt of the Elites*, a collection of short essays published posthumously in 1995, Lasch extends and deepens his exploration of the possibility of a democratic populism and of a "new wisdom of limits." Lasch argues that we need to update Ortega's famous notion of "the revolt of the masses," the masses being a new kind of multitude who combine "radical ingratitude with an unquestioned belief in limitless possibility" (1995, p. 40). They celebrate specialization and technical expertise and are concerned mainly to rise in the modern meritocracy. But such meritocracy is a "parody of democracy" and—here Lasch (1991, p. 41) quotes R. H. Tawney in his 1924 book interestingly entitled *Equality*—"'its opportunities to rise are no substitute for a general diffusion of the means of civilization,' of the 'dignity and culture' that are needed by all 'whether they rise or not.'" Today, however, the greatest threat to democracy and civilization Lasch suggests comes from social and economic *elites* who retain most of the wealth and income, have themselves little or no sense of history or indebtedness to it, identify with no particular nation or community, and enjoy a "global bazaar" far from the madding crowd and entirely out of touch with ordinary working folk.

Lasch argues that one of the eminently human and decent things that gets erased in a brave new world of a global bazaar with many left behind is what Oldenburg (1989) calls "great good places,"[6] neighborhood hangouts and informal meeting places that have given way to shopping malls. They are "third places," different from highly structured organizations or families and other small groups. They also differ greatly from clubs, political affiliations, or online social networks based on shared tastes, personal inclination, or political biases. They are uniquely rewarding and beneficial but are rapidly disappearing from the scene. In Oldenburg's view, the "open agenda of rambling third place conversations" promotes "habits of decency" that spill over into the wider community. Lasch (1995, p. 119) summarizes Oldenburg's idea: at their best, "'[W]hatever hint of a hierarchy exists in such places is predicated upon human decency' and not on wealth, glamour, aggression, or even intelligence."

Lasch (1995) suggests that the best account of the neighborhood's political potential is still Mary Parker Follett's book *The New State*, published in 1918. She, too, explains how the sociability of neighborhoods (in contrast to that of typical "voluntary associations") causes decency to be "more highly regarded in the third place than wealth or brilliant achievement" and regularly "deflates the balloon of pomposity and pretension." In this and other ways it encourages essential political virtues (pp. 121–122).

Democratic Populism and the "Lost Art of Argument"

In *Revolt of the Elites*, Lasch (1995) spells out further some of what would be involved in a genuine democratic populism. Above all, it requires "wide-ranging, free-wheeling conversation" (p. 117), exemplified by both wide open, uncensored neighborhood exchanges and the "[candid] . . . pungent, colloquial, sometimes racy" Lincoln-Douglass debates of 1858.[7]

In Lasch's (1995) telling, the scandals of the Gilded Age (about 1870 to 1890) led the educated classes in the U.S. to advocate for a professionalization of both politics and journalism that sterilized them as much as it reformed them. One of the villains in this movement in the early twentieth century was Walter Lippman (1889–1974), who distrusted public opinion, thought the role of the press should be to "circulate information, not . . . encourage argument," and argued that while the public would care about the outcomes of lawmaking, the substance of it should be left to knowledgeable experts whose principles as much as possible grew out of "disinterested scientific inquiry. . . . [E]verything else was ideology" (pp. 168–169). But this only means that the public then "has no reason to inform itself about civic affairs" because "people readily acquire [only] such knowledge as they can put to good use" (p. 162). Hence the much-lamented decline of interest in and knowledge about public affairs among the citizenry.

However, according to Lasch (1995), "What democracy requires is vigorous public debate," (p. 162), above all with those with whom we have serious disagreements. In the view of hermeneutic moral realism or interpretive social science (Bishop, 2007; Richardson et al., 1999), Lipmann's sharp "epistemological distinction between truth and mere opinion" (Lasch, 1995, p. 169) is particularly unhelpful. It manages to simultaneously embrace the errors of both "subjectivism" and "objectivism" that Slife and Yanchar (this volume, p. 22) delineate. The "coming-to-understanding" (Taylor, 2002) within and between us that is the heartbeat of human existence concerns meanings that do not resemble natural scientific findings nor can be counted as mere subjective opinion or whimsy. They involve the interplay of convictions and ideals that form the crux of our identity but are never final or certain and require correction or improvement from different—sometimes annoyingly different!—others. Ontological hermeneutics and Bakhtin's dialogism clarify aspects of this process and its central place in human existence. But it would be hard to find a better account of its core dynamic than this passage from *Revolt of the Elites*:

> it is the act of articulating and defending our views that lifts them out of the category of "opinion" . . . we come to know our own minds only by explaining our selves to others. . . . The attempt to bring others around to our own point of view carries the risk, of course, that we may adopt their point of view instead. We have to enter imaginatively into our opponents' arguments, if only for the purpose of refuting them, and we may end up being persuaded by those we sought to persuade. Argument is risky and unpredictable, therefore educational. Most of us tend to think of it (as Lippman thought of it) as a clash of rival dogmas, a shouting match in which neither side gives any ground. But arguments are won by changing opponents' minds—something that can only happen if we give [them] a respectful hearing and still persuade

their advocates that there is something wrong with those arguments. In the course of this activity we may well decide that there is something wrong with our own.

(1995, pp. 170–171)

Search for a New Wisdom of Limits

In the last few chapters of *The Revolt of the Elites*, Lasch (1995) deepens his reflections about the "forbidden topic" and need for a "new wisdom" of limits, without which progress in the direction of democratic populism is unlikely to occur. Such wisdom would encourage more modest standards of living that were in accord with the values of a great many ordinary Americans who know that one can't have everything and that everything comes at a cost. Lasch objects to the way that political ideologies peddle "optimism" about an unending improvement that is out of touch with ordinary people's lives and fails elites, as well, in the end. In its place he cautiously recommends not optimism but "hope," hope for a meaningful life that might come in spite of, or better incorporates, indelible human limits (Elshtain, 1999). In a remarkable passage, Lasch (1995) writes:

> As Hannah Arendt has pointed out, The Enlightenment got it backward. It is citizenship that confers equality, not equality that creates a right to citizenship. Sameness is not equality, and "political equality, therefore, is the very opposite of the equality before death," Arendt says, ". . . or of equality before God." Political equality—citizenship—equalizes people who are otherwise unequal in their capacities, and the universalization of citizenship therefore has to be accompanied not only by formal training in the civic arts but by measures designed to assure the broadest distribution of economic and political responsibility. . . .
>
> (p. 88)

What is equality before death or God? Essentially, in part, it is human finitude, a condition we all share. It involves a wildly unequal distribution of abilities, talents, and conventionally desirable qualities along with all the pain, confusion, and envy that engenders. It is a condition of mortality and impending death. It entails much disappointment, painful ethical conflicts, some degree of suffering, susceptibility to tragedy and loss, and the necessity of trying to find meaning and purpose in living even though much of life remains a mystery. These are among the "limits" concerning which we suppose Lasch believes we need greater wisdom, something hard to come by in a culture of "optimism" that places most of its bets on "endless improvement."

In a chapter entitled "The Abolition of Shame," Lasch (1995) deepens his analysis of how we obscure human limits and the price we pay for doing so. He sharply critiques the tendency in much post-Freudian psychology, both professional and "pop," to downplay and whitewash "intrapsychic conflict." He fully appreciates the problems with Freud's metapsychology (or at least many of them), including its problematic determinism and patriarchal overtones. He seeks an alternative to partly outmoded Freudian theory and the shallow trends that mostly have succeeded it, one that places deep human conflicts and struggle with ultimately insurmountable human limits at the center of the picture.

An example of the problem is the widespread tendency "to define shame" as simply "the absence of self-esteem" (Lasch, 1995, p. 198). Many schools of thought claim to bring shame out of the dark and expose it as something pointlessly judgmental, moralistic, reflective of an "outmoded prudery, and only harmful to self-actualization and a fulfilling life." Some of these accounts extend the critique to the wider society and its punishing norms and even make society itself the patient (Frank, 1948; Nichols, 1991), a view leading them to encourage the advance of a number of human rights and an expansion of the welfare state. Thus they fit hand in glove with the aims of "progressive neoliberalism" (Fraser, 2017). Moreover, Lasch points out, they do a fine job of deflecting people's attention away from gross economic inequalities and the absence of genuine democratic politics.

Lasch (1995) cites the work of the psychiatrist and theorist Leon Wurmser (1981) in his book *The Mask of Shame* as providing a deeper and more credible account of the dynamics of shame. Wurmser finds that often in the experience of shame in severe psychopathology there are "archaic conflicts" that grow out of the "conflict of union and separateness," the conflict between an urge to "merge symbiotically with the world" and to "become absolutely self-sufficient." Also there is, he finds, both an effort "to hide from the world" and "to penetrate its secrets" (Lasch, 1995, p. 201). Lasch writes,

> The record of [this] suffering makes us see why shame is so closely associated with the body, which resists efforts to control it and therefore reminds us, vividly and painfully, of our inescapable limitations, the inescapability of death above everything. It is man's bondage to nature, as Erich Heller once said, that makes him ashamed.

Thus shame can hardly be abolished, for it is something endemic to the human condition. Still, there may be a way of living with or transforming life within these limits and inescapable, difficult conflicts. Lasch (1995) says that "Wurmser pleads for the 'heroic transcendence of shame' through love and work" (p. 201). This seems to imply a "search for meaning" that digs a lot deeper and represents a much more ethically or spiritually challenging effort that just conferring equality or granting or claiming human rights. Without it, sadly, Lasch is telling us, democratic populism may not be possible.

Notes

1. An example might be the sense of happiness and pride and that parents enjoy when their child shows empathy for others or follows their conscience even though it risks disappointment or disapproval from others (regardless of the child's worldly accomplishments), compared with finding their primary satisfaction or reward in their child's competitive achievement in academics, athletics, or questing for greater prestige or popularity (even if the child follow norms of honesty and fair play in reaching those goals).
2. Erich Fromm (1941/69) identified some key aspects of this situation in a pungent manner over eighty years ago, He argues that we have a well-developed sense of "freedom from" arbitrary authority and from dogmatic or irrational impediments to freedom and to exercising greater control over nature and ourselves. However, we sorely lack a corresponding sense of "freedom to" or "freedom for" that would give some context, direction, or deeper purpose to our increased freedom and opportunity.
3. The term liberal individualism refers to broad premises about life and living that are shared by both so-called political "liberals" and "conservatives" today. Both make individuals and individual autonomy or rights the cornerstone of their approach, even though they disagree about what those essential rights are, and both tend to rely on large-scale impersonal mechanisms, either the state or market or both in varying ways to sort out our differences
4. Alasdair McIntyre (1981) in *After Virtue* makes a similar point. With the notion of "bureaucratic individualism," he points out how expanded voluntarist autonomy requires an ever greater bureaucratic state apparatus to defend rights and resolve conflicts.
5. McWilliams (2016, p. 14) notes that much of this was personal for Lasch, born of his concern for his own children's future. "Lasch realized that his children were growing up in a society where naked ambition and the willingness to get ahead at all costs count more than honest, devoted, productive work."
6. The snazzy title of Ray Oldenburg's (1989) book is *The Great Good Places: Cafés, Coffee Shops, Community Centers, Beauty Parlors, General Stores, Bars, Hangouts and How They Get You Through the Day*. Of course, they can also be the scene of bias, prejudice, shallowness, and pettiness. But they often rise above them, as well. Such is life.
7. A series of seven debates, drawing as many as 15,000 people.

References

Bakhtin, M. (1981). *The dialogical imagination: Four essays by M. M. Bakhtin.* (M. Holquist, Ed.). Austin: University of Texas Press.

Bellah, R., Madsen, R., Sullivan, W., Swindler, A., & Tipton, S. (1985). *Habits of the heart: Individualism and commitment in American life*. Berkeley, CA: University of California Press.

Bishop, R. C. (2007). *The philosophy of the social sciences*. New York, NY: Continuum.

Brill, S. (2018). *Tailspin: The people and forces behind America's fifty-year fall—and those fighting to reverse it*. New York: Knopf.

Brinkman, S. (2010). *Perspectives on normativity*. New York: Springer.

Brown, W. (2003). Neo-liberalism and the end of liberal democracy. *Theory & Event, 7*. Retrieved from http://muse.jhu.edu.ezproxy.lib.utexas.edu/

Chen, V. (2016, December). The spiritual crisis of the modern economy. *Atlantic*. Retrieved from www.theatlantic.com/business/archive/2016/12/spiritual-crisis-modern-economy/511067/

Cushman, P. (1990). Why the self is empty. *American Psychologist, 45*, 599–611.

Davies, B., & Bansel, P. (2007). Neoliberalism and education. *International Journal of Qualitative Studies in Education, 20*, 247–259. doi:10.1080/0951839070128175

Deneen, P. (2018). *Why liberalism failed*. New Haven: Yale University Press.

Deresiewicz, W. (2014a, July 21). Don't send your kid to the Ivy League. *The New Republic*. https://newrepublic.com/article/118747/ivy-league-schools-are-overrated-send-your-kids-elsewhere

Deresiewicz, W. (2014b). *Excellent sheep: The miseducation of the American elite*. New York: The Free Press.

Elshtain, J. (1999). Limits and hope: Christopher Lasch and political theory. *Social Research, 66*, 531–543.

Foucault, M. (2008). *The birth of biopolitics: Lectures at the Collège de France 1978–1979*. Basingstoke, UK: Palgrave Macmillan. doi:10.1057/9780230594180

Fraser, N. (2017, January 2). The end of progressive neoliberalism. *Dissent*. https://www.dissentmagazine.org/online_articles/progressive-neoliberalism-reactionary-populism-nancy-fraser

Gadamer, H.-G. (1989). *Truth and method* (2nd rev. ed., J. Weinsheimer and D. Marshall, Trans.). New York: Crossroad.

Gergen, K. (1985). The social constructionist movement in modern psychology. *American Psychologist, 40*, 266–275.

Harvey, D. (2005). *A brief history of neoliberalism*. New York: Oxford University Press.

Heidegger, M. (1962). *Being and time*. New York: Harper and Row.

Lasch, C. (1991). *The true and only heaven: Progress and its critics*. New York: W. W. Norton.

Lasch, C. (1995). *The revolt of the elites and the betrayal of democracy*. New York: W. W. Norton.

Lears, J. (2015, April 20). The liberal arts vs. Neoliberalism. *Commonweal Magazine*.

Lilla, M. (2014). The truth about our libertarian age: Why the dogma of democracy doesn't always make the world better. *New Republic, 17*: https://newrepublic.com/article/118043/our-libertarian-age-dogma-democracy-dogma-decline.

Liu, E., & Hanauer, N. (2011). *The gardens of democracy*. Seattle, WA: Sasquatch Books.

MacIntyre, A. (1981). *After virtue*. Notre Dame, Paris: University of Notre Dame Press.

Martin, J., & McLellan, A. (2013). *The education of selves: How psychology transformed students*. New York: Oxford University Press. Retrieved from http://dx.doi.org/10.1093/acprof:oso/9780199913671.001.0001

McWilliams, S. (2016, Fall). The true and only Lasch: On the true and only heaven 25 years later. *Modern Age Journal*, 11–17.

Mills, M. (2016, March). In defense of populism. *First Things*. Retrieved from www.firstthings.com/web-exclusives/2016/03/in-defense-of-populism

Oldenburg, R. (1989). *The great good place*. New York: Marlowe & Company.

Richardson, F. C., Bishop, R. C., & Garcia-Joslin, J. (2018). Overcoming neoliberalism. *Journal of Theoretical and Philosophical Psychology*, *38*(1), 15–28. http://dx.doi.org/10.1037/teo0000071

Richardson, F. C., Fowers, B., & Guignon, C. (1999). *Re-envisioning psychology: Moral dimensions of theory and practice*. San Francisco, CA: Jossey-Bass.

Rorty, R. (1982). *Consequences of pragmatism*. Minneapolis: University of Minnesota Press.

Rose, N. (1999). *Governing the soul: The shaping of the private self* (2nd ed.). London, UK: Free Association Books.

Sandel, M. (1996). *Democracy's discontent: America in search of a public philosophy*. Cambridge, MA: Harvard University Press.

Selznick, P. (1992). *The moral commonwealth*. Berkeley, CA: University of California Press.

Sennett, R. (1998). *The corrosion of character: The personal consequences of work in the new capitalism*. New York: Norton.

Sewall, G. (2016, April). Donald Trump and the ghost of Christopher Lasch. *The American Conservative*. Retrieved from www.theamericanconservative.com/articles/donald-trump-and-the-ghost-of-christopher-lasch/

Slife, B., Smith, A., & Burchfield, C. (2003). Psychotherapists as crypto-missionaries: An exemplar on the crossroads of history, theory, and philosophy. In D. Hill & M. Krall (Eds.), *About psychology: At the crossroads of history, theory, and philosophy*. Albany, NY: State University of New York Press.

Stewart, M. (2018, June). The 9.9 percent is the new American aristocracy. *The Atlantic*. Retrieved from www.theatlantic.com/magazine/archive/2018/06/the-birth-of-a-new-american-aristocracy/559130/

Stoller, M. (2016, October). How democrats killed their populist soul. *Atlantic*. Retrieved from www.theatlantic.com/politics/archive/2016/10/how-democrats-killed-their-populist-soul/504710/

Sugarman, J. (2013, October). *Neoliberalism and the ethics of psychology*. Paper presented at the Psychology and the Other Conference, Cambridge, MA.

Sugarman, J. (2015). Neoliberalism and psychological ethics. *Journal of Theoretical and Philosophical Psychology*, *35*, 103–116.

Sugarman, J. (2018). *Neoliberalism is taking a steep toll on an entire generation's mental health: Study*. Retrieved from www.alternet.org/news-amp-politics/neoliberalism-taking-steep-toll-entire-generations-mental-health-study

Sullivan, A. (2017, April 30). The reactionary temptation. *New York Magazine.* Retrieved from http://nymag.com/daily/intelligencer/2017/04/andrew-sullivan-why-the-reactionary-right-must-be-taken-seriously.html

Sullivan, W. (1986). *Reconstructing public philosophy.* Berkeley, CA: University of California Press.

Taylor, C. (1985). Interpretation and the sciences of man. In C. Taylor, *Philosophy and the human sciences: Philosophical papers* (Vol. 2, pp. 15–57). Cambridge, MA: Cambridge University Press.

Taylor, C. (1989). *Sources of the self.* Cambridge, MA: Harvard University Press.

Taylor, C. (2002). Gadamer and the human sciences. In R. Dostal (Ed.), *The Cambridge companion to Gadamer* (pp. 126–142). Cambridge: Cambridge University Press.

Tocqueville, A. de. (1969). *Democracy in America.* New York: Anchor Books. (Original work published 1835)

Wurmser, L. (1981). *The mask of shame.* New York: Rowman & Littlefield.

Yeats, W. (1952). The second coming. In O. Williams (Ed.), *Immortal poems of the English language* (p. 489). New York: Washington Square Press.

7 Inquiry Into Moral Configurations

Stephen C. Yanchar and Susan Peterson Gong

This chapter provides an overview and example of research based on a hermeneutic moral realist interpretive frame. To clarify what a study of this sort might entail, we will describe a recent investigation of student question asking in a graduate seminar on design thinking. This study focused on how classroom questioning among students showed up—that is, its purposes, significance, dynamics, affordances, complexities, and so forth—when it was taken to occur within a morally configured space of practice. As we present this example study, we will outline the hermeneutic moral realist interpretive frame that informed our approach, describe the investigative process we undertook, and present a subset of findings concerned with virtuous (or not so virtuous) ways of asking questions. This subset of findings, and others we generated (summarized in the following), suggest how student questioning was entangled within a complex configuration of temporally situated moral demands, expectations, and relationships. Given our hermeneutic commitments, we do not present our approach as canonical; rather, we present it as one way to perform inquiry from this perspective. There are surely others.

An Interpretive Frame: Assumptions and Emphases

What we offer can be seen as an extension of prior arguments regarding hermeneutic moral realism as a basis for inquiry (Brinkmann, 2011; Stigliano, 1990; Yanchar & Slife, 2017; for the philosophical roots of this perspective, see Hatab, 2000; Smith, 2002; Taylor, 1989). While this general position has been advanced primarily in theoretical terms to this point, we offer a concrete sense of how one might perform this kind of investigation and what its findings might look like. Before we offer this example, however, we briefly summarize several of its key assumptions.

Hermeneutic moral realist theory suggests that human life is predominantly characterized by engagement in practices, and that to understand the meaning of some phenomenon—that is, how the phenomenon matters in human life—one must consider its fit within the context of practice. But a practice, from this perspective, involves more than simply participating in a certain role or engaging in regularly patterned activities; it involves ontologically real (i.e., out there in the world) moral demands that bring meaning and direction regarding how one may participate.

These ontologically real moral demands can, for analytical purposes, be differentiated into two kinds. First are *practice-internal goods*, which are the intrinsic outcomes of correct engagement in a given practice (e.g., a good of being a physician is healing). Second are *moral "reference points"* (Smith, 2002, p. 97) that provide some indication of how those goods may be effectively and virtuously brought about (e.g., a good physician is, among other things, a good listener). In this sense, any practice involves conduct that is expected and, indeed, exemplary, in the pursuit of its goods; it provides moral points of orientation regarding not only what one should accomplish, but also, generally speaking, how one should go about it. And the complex ecologies of practice granted meaning by these goods and reference points we refer to as *moral configurations*.

Moral configurations that form the space of practice are part of the banality of existence. They constitute the everyday world of human action and thus the medium in which life is lived. Although explicit moral dilemmas sometimes arise in the midst of practice, and constitute an important topic of inquiry, from this hermeneutic perspective the breadth of the moral is more encompassing than the momentous, yet relatively infrequent, dilemmas often studied in psychological research. Thus, the term *moral*, from this hermeneutic perspective, emphasizes the everyday ways in which people engage in practices and strive (or fail to strive) to pursue practice-internal goods, guided by expectations for correct action implicit within them. If these everyday moral configurations are as significant as we contend here, then they warrant scholarly attention and should somehow be foregrounded in the conduct of inquiry.

The interpretive frame that guided our study, based on this moral realist body of theorizing, entails four principal emphases:

- The *moral significance* of the phenomenon being investigated, which concerns how it matters or makes a difference in the moral space of the practice in question.
- *Practice-internal goods* (the intrinsic outcome of practice) and *reference points* (guiding expectations, standards, values) that provide a morally configured space in which the target phenomenon can matter and the goods of practice can be pursued in better or worse ways, or perhaps not pursued at all.

- *Moral becoming*, which concerns participants' changing familiarity with the target phenomenon over the course of their practical involvement with it, in the midst of a given practice's moral configurations (i.e., a phenomenon's moral fit into their past, present, and a projected future).
- *Moral complexities*, which are the tensions, binds, paradoxes, and so forth that accompany participation in the moral configurations of a given practice.

Taken together, these four emphases provide a framework for inquiry into moral configurations, irrespective of any particular research strategy one might adopt; they provide the interpretive basis upon which a phenomenon can show up as mattering in the practical-moral sense that we have described here (for more on this interpretive frame, see Yanchar & Slife, 2017).

This interpretive frame rests on a number of other, more general hermeneutic contentions as well, based primarily on the work of Heidegger (1962) and Gadamer (1989). We briefly summarize the most obvious and significant ones here.

- *Situated participation*, in which human involvement is fully embodied, often tacit, and fundamentally embedded in immanently meaningful, historically situated contexts of participation, thus forming a unitary agency-world phenomenon.
- *Possibility*, which exists in the world of practice itself. People, objects, events, spaces of participation, and so on have possibilities; they show up in a myriad of ways, or not at all, depending on one's practical involvement with them.
- *Temporality*, in which past, present, and future exist as co-aspects of a fundamental unity; possibilities show up in an open-ended future to be projected into and a past that is subject to reconstrual in light of present considerations and future projections.
- *Interpretation*, which concerns unconcealment or explication of what was hitherto tacit, forgotten, or vaguely perceived; and along with any unconcealment is the implication that something else lies simultaneously concealed. Interpretation occurs in explicit attempts to explore phenomena and in everyday (tacit) projecting and pressing into possibilities.
- *Concernful involvement*, in which people's participation reflects what matters to them and the intrinsic meaning of in-the-world circumstances; concernful involvement functions as a kind of embodied commentary or self-interpretation regarding what is worth pursuing, how one should manage the affairs of life, and so on.

- *Participational agency* (Yanchar, 2011), which, as a general concept, focalizes the foregoing assumptions into a single account of human existence. Participational agents are situated, fully embodied, concernfully involved, temporally constituted, interpreting beings enmeshed (often tacitly) in a world of participation and possibility.

The Inquiry Process

Inquiry based on this interpretive frame is designed to investigate the fit of a target phenomenon (i.e., its purposes, significance, dynamics, affordances, complexities, etc.) within the moral configurations of a given practice. The general purpose of this case study, then, was to answer the question: what is revealed about graduate student question asking, and about the practice of being a graduate student in this classroom setting, when examined from a moral realist standpoint? Through this approach we generated a two-fold set of findings which includes first, a description of the specific classroom context and, second, a set of themes regarding its practical-moral significance.

From a hermeneutic perspective, these findings are best thought of as a *shared understanding* between researchers and participants. While our study was clearly dependent upon our efforts and interpretations, it was also dependent upon participants' willingness to be observed, to be interviewed, and to offer feedback on our findings. We thus saw our study as based on a unique, inquiry-oriented collaboration that is common to qualitative research.

Ultimately, our goal was to answer our research questions in ways that would yield transferable insight (Lincoln & Guba, 1985). We did not seek to provide an impartial mapping of moral terrain or adduce universal moral principles. Rather, our goal was to provide a contextual disclosure of question asking within moral configurations of graduate student practice in ways that might be illuminating to others.

Assumption Clarification

Throughout the study we sought to clarify our assumptions about question asking as a part of graduate student practice in this domain. To do this, we specified our basic hermeneutic contentions delineated above, in addition to those pertaining to questioning per se as a form of class involvement. This process was facilitated by reviewing scholarly literature in which question asking was conceptualized from a number of perspectives. Based on our hermeneutic commitments, and in contrast to other views in the literature (e.g., cognitive and logic-centered; see Gong, 2018, for a review), we developed a set of assumptions which, in summary, took question asking to be an expression of one's participational agency in the pursuit of learning. The inquiry that followed, then, served to deepen, broaden, and clarify this initial assumptive background.

Case Selection

The case we selected for this study was a graduate seminar on design thinking in the college of education at a major university. We made this selection based on several criteria. For our research questions, which focused on graduate student question asking, the class needed to: 1) be graduate level; 2) provide ample opportunity for student question asking and discussion; and 3) include diverse student backgrounds with respect to tenure and experience in a design field. Since the class size was relatively small, two women and six men (one of whom was the instructor), we used no particular selection criteria for individual participants and all members agreed to participate.

Data Collection

Given our interest in the fit of student questions within the actual (morally configured) practice of being a graduate student, we collected and triangulated several different data types, including class artifacts, class observations, and in-depth, semi-structured interviews. Artifacts included the course syllabus, several assignments, student responses to assignments, and personal writings of students. Classroom observations (recorded and later transcribed) were conducted by one member of the research team (SPG) who attended eight class sessions spanning four weeks and took field notes. Finally we conducted three semi-structured interviews per student and two with the instructor (each lasting approximately one hour).

Questions were developed for each interview as the study progressed. The purpose of the first interview was to get to know participants and their ways of engaging in classroom learning in general, with a focus on question asking. The second interview focused on question-asking interactions that took place in the classroom itself, as well as relevant issues that came up in interview 1. The third interview followed up on discussions from the first two interviews and explored participants' reactions to initial themes we were developing at that time. The first two interviews for each participant were conducted by one of us alone (SPG); the third interview for each participant we conducted together, as we had each formulated unique follow-up questions for participants at this point in the study.

Finally, we interviewed the instructor only twice. The first interview focused on his views of student question asking (from an instructor's perspective), and the second focused on specific episodes from class, his thoughts on our developing themes, and any other relevant issues not yet discussed. Again, the instructor's first interview was conducted by one of us alone (SPG); the second interview we conducted jointly.

Data Analysis

Prior to interviews, one of us (SPG) analyzed artifacts, field notes, class recordings, and class transcripts in order to gain initial familiarity with the class context and phenomena related to question asking. This involved a re-iterative review, comparison, and contrast of these data sources as a form of triangulation, allowing us to arrive at a clear sense of classroom proceedings and interactions. This analysis provided a basis for the interviews that followed, as many interview questions (especially in interview 2) were concerned with actual classroom dynamics related to question asking.

We analyzed interviews independently so we could each develop our own sense of the data; we then merged our tentative findings later in the process (as described next), thus engaging in a kind of co-interpretation. We analyzed interview 1 for each participant before conducting interview 2 (to the point of "initial thematizing;" see more on this in the following), and analyzed interview 2 for each participant before conducting interview 3. Although we performed our analyses separately, we used the same overall data analytic strategy, which included the following phases.

Coding

We first sought general familiarity with the transcripts by carefully reading them and performing initial coding of how question asking mattered in the moral context of practice for our participants. Prior to analysis we created a set of initial codes to help identify and interpret relevant phenomena in the context of practice itself or in participants' reflections on practice. Thus, each code could pertain to specific instances of phenomena in the classroom or more general reflections. Our codes were as follows:

- **P**: Practical involvement with the target phenomenon—what participants did in class, how they asked questions, impressions of others' questions, and so on.
- **S**: Strivings and self-evaluations—what students hoped to achieve in class and the role that questions played in their pursuits; also how students assessed their own efforts in these respects.
- **V**: Value judgments—students' statements of ought, good and bad, better or worse, and so on.

- **E**: Enablements—what question asking enabled with respect to student participation and striving.
- **H**: Hindrances—what question asking hindered with respect to student participation and striving.
- **F**: Facilitation—what facilitated student question asking.
- **I**: Impediments—what impeded student question asking.
- **T**: Tensions and balances—tensions among goods, reference points, and so on with respect to question asking; also how students sought to cope with these tensions; other complexities that showed up as relevant in class (e.g., significant ambiguities, ironies, paradoxes, etc.).
- **O**: Other relevant phenomena that don't fit the above codes.

Using these codes at this early stage allowed us to foreground student question asking within the moral space of class practice and helped us maintain a hermeneutic moral realist perspective throughout the data analysis. After this initial coding, we reread the transcripts to achieve greater familiarity and revised or added codes as needed. We then created expanded codes by supplementing each initial code with a more specific, contextual description or meaning. For example, one of us initially coded a passage from the interview transcripts as H and V, and then later added the following expanded code: "Class time taken up with people questioning and disagreeing, but no edification as a result." In this instance, the participant made an observation about an episode in class that was initially coded as both "hindrance" and a "value judgment;" our expanded code then offered more contextual meaning.

Thematizing

We formulated initial themes by grouping together expanded codes that appeared to be related in significant ways. Some initial themes were: "questions blocked by dominant voices," "questions that reveal misunderstanding, lack of knowledge, or lack of preparation," and "would rather discuss or engage in other activities at times, not all question asking." Of these three, only the first was finally retained as a theme; the other two were eventually integrated into others.

Inferring

We made initial inferences about what appeared to be moral reference points and practice-internal goods of practice in this setting, as well as tensions among them. For example, some initial inferences concerned possible reference points such as "personal growth," "be a good listener," and "adequate preparation." Practice-internal goods were less visible and more broad; there was a general, but rarely articulated, sense among participants that the purpose of design study as a practice was to pursue competence or excellence as a designer; thus, becoming a designer—or variations on this theme—was more or less the implicit good of participation in this seminar. Other initial inferences had to do with tensions and balances, for example, students striking an appropriate contextual balance between asking questions vs. allowing others to contribute. We integrated these inferences into the themes we were developing, in order to give them greater richness and to more clearly foreground the moral configurations within which question asking took place.

Refined Thematizing

After all three interviews had been conducted for each participant, and each interview had been analyzed to the point of making inferences, we began refining initial themes and inferences into more refined themes (by merging, splitting, adding, deleting, editing, etc.). For example, one refined theme that we present below concerned "virtuous question asking." As we refined themes we also explored possible interrelations among all that we were observing (e.g., various themes, goods, reference points, tensions, and so forth) by engaging in part-part and part-whole analysis (asking ourselves, for example, "How are these two reference points connected?" or "How does this reference point guide toward the broader good of practice?"). This interrelating activity enabled us to further refine themes, identify possible subthemes or metathemes, and consider how they might all fit into a single thematic structure.

Structuring

After we each separately developed a set of refined themes, we considered them jointly as a single body of possible findings. At this point, we worked together to iteratively develop them into a final thematic structure by formulating what we took to be an internally consistent and illuminating set of insights. This overall thematic structure can be seen, hermeneutically, as a refinement of our initial, assumptive sense of the target phenomenon. However, it is also important to note that we strived to be open to, and surprised by, the phenomena as they presented themselves to us; we did not predict most of the specific insights enabled by our use of this interpretive frame in this context.

Trustworthiness

From our first efforts to design this study through completion we sought to maintain acceptable standards of trustworthiness, as described by Lincoln and Guba (1985). To this end, we conducted progressive subjectivity checks, peer debriefing, persistent observation, data triangulation, negative case analysis, and member checking.

Example Findings

Case Description

To provide an overview of the context in which this study took place, we formulated a description of everyday student participation in the seminar. Space constraints do not permit us to provide a detailed account here, but this description included the physical setting of the classroom, ordinary class proceedings, the general nature of interactions among students and with the instructor, student questioning, and student participation leading up to the final project at the end of the term (for a more detailed description, see Gong, 2018).

Overall Thematic Structure

The findings that we eventually developed were based primarily on interview data, though supplemented significantly by analyses of observations and artifacts (as noted above). Our eventual thematic structure entailed seven themes organized according to three metathemes.

Metatheme 1, entitled "questions in the complexity of practice," emphasized various reference points that showed up in this classroom setting and the moral stances, so to speak, that participants took on those reference points by way of their questioning.

Metatheme 2, entitled "the sociality of question asking," emphasized how questions showed up in the moral configurations of practice for these participants and the complexities that participants' faced in their relationships with other students as they sought to navigate the configurations of this setting.

Metatheme 3, entitled "the temporality of questions in practice," emphasized how reference points and goods were situated in a temporal unity of past, present, and future, and how students' current ways of participating (including question asking) were often tied to reference points encountered in prior classroom experiences. This metatheme also emphasized how some previously encountered reference points, in tension with current ones, were reinterpretable in light of students' present concerns and future projections. (The complete body of findings can be found in Gong, 2018.)

One Example Theme

As an example, we offer an abridged version of one of our themes—virtuous question asking. In this theme we suggest how questioning for these participants (using pseudonyms) was implicated in what might be thought of as virtuous classroom conduct. We chose to present this theme here because it was, in our estimation, the least complex of the seven themes we formulated and thus the easiest to present in a condensed form.

One pattern in our data concerned humility, sincerity, and honesty in question asking—virtues that showed up as reference points regarding how students ought to pursue the academic goods of practice in the class. We thus saw how participants were led toward or away from the goods of graduate student practice in this setting by way of these virtues; that is, how their questioning qua agentic striving served as a commentary on these moral reference points.

In this regard, questions were deeply connected with character and how to be a good question asker as a student in this seminar. For example, students suggested that humility was an inherent part of true questioning, or "humility is huge" as one student noted. Jacky and Dr. Smith both suggested at least one reason why this is so, when they saw humility as pointing toward greater learning, discovery, and openness. According to Dr. Smith, the humility of question asking was "related to the question, *do the students really feel a sincere desire to learn?*" For Jacky, this desire included considerations of honesty and openness, "We are willing to ask a true question when we are humble."

Jim made a connection between honesty, humility, and equality:

> Having constructive conversation requires humility in order to see what the other person is thinking, and your question should be like a bridge between perspectives beneficial to you, but also mean something to the other person. . . . Humility and equality and honesty, not only learning from them, but contributing to them.

Peter's version of humility was similar, a recognition of the value of the contribution of others:

> In a way, I think that humility is kind of inescapable, because to learn something . . . *I now know something that I didn't before*, I have to kind of assent to that being the case. . . . It's something that I didn't come up with, something that I learned from somebody else. . . . And there's a kind of deference in that, at a very basic fundamental level.

Although participants' comments suggest reference points such as honesty, sincerity, and humility, most students in the seminar admitted to having participated in questioning interchanges that did not quite live up to those expectations. For some, a question might actually be a way of asserting one's opinion, but in a way that appears sufficiently modest. As Harry and Peter both suggested, sometimes their own answers were couched within their questions. For these participants at least, it appears that presenting one's claim in the form of a question comes off more humbly and less brashly; and to be brash would be to violate a reference point regarding how one conducts oneself in this type of setting.

When queried on this issue, Dr. Smith discussed a related phenomenon:

> There is a norm that students are not going to showboat, . . . I think if students feel that another student is showboating or trying to monopolize or draw attention to them or their views, I think that they tend to react poorly to that.

Although Peter suggested that this kind of "impression management for its own sake is low," he admitted to having asked questions as a way to impress others. Several students identified these kinds of questions as "posturing," where the communication might be in the form of a question, but the intent would be to convey something other than the apparent content of the question—for example, one's own wealth of knowledge or insight.

Whether or not these participants queried in virtuous ways at any given time, their awareness of this issue highlights moral demands regarding how students should stand in relationship to each other and the good of the class. Although layered and nuanced, a more or less right and wrong way to participate as a question asker became apparent in this class setting. And what might be seen as virtues—for example, humility, sincerity, and honesty—operated in the background as reference points regarding student questioning, and how the goods of classroom practice, in this setting, could be appropriately pursued.

Conclusion

These findings—albeit in condensed form—provide some insight into question asking and the moral configurations of graduate student practice in this class setting. Surely there can be no single, all-encompassing summary of their significance. But they do suggest, among other things, that questioning is more complex than a mere cognitive act or even a social act per se; it involves moral-practical considerations that appear to be interwoven into anything that might be considered cognitive, social, or whatever else. At least for these participants, sincere question asking enabled good learning for oneself and others, while insincerity counted as a kind of moral transgression and possible occlusion in pursuit of the good. The value of findings like these can be determined by consumers of this research, but they may provide suggestions regarding how students can be invited to query in more helpful ways, for all involved, and thus how to promote a more edifying class environment. Insights of this type, of course, would supplement those regarding the practice of classroom learning per se and how it might be fruitfully investigated.

References

Brinkmann, S. (2011). *Psychology as a moral science: Perspectives on normativity.* New York: Springer.

Gadamer, H. G. (1989). *Truth and method* (2nd rev. ed.). New York: Continuum.

Gong, S. P. (2018). *Student question-asking: Interpreting the moral ecology of class-room practice* (Unpublished dissertation). Brigham Young University, Provo, UT.

Hatab, L. (2000). *Ethics and finitude: Heidegggerian contributions to moral philosophy.* Lanham, MD: Rowman & Littlefield.

Heidegger, M. (1962). *Being and time.* New York: Harper and Row.

Lincoln, Y. S., & Guba, E. G. (1985). *Naturalistic inquiry* (pp. 289–331). Newbury Park, CA: Sage Publications.

Smith, N. H. (2002). *Charles Taylor: Meaning, morals, and modernity.* Malden, MA: Polity Press.

Stigliano, A. (1990). The moral basis of human science. *Saybrook Review, 8*(1), 73–104.

Taylor, C. (1989). *Sources of the self: The making of the modern identity.* Cambridge, MA: Harvard University Press.

Yanchar, S. C. (2011). Participational agency. *Review of General Psychology, 15*(3), 277–287.

Yanchar, S. C., & Slife, B. D. (2017). Theorizing inquiry in the moral space of practice. *Qualitative Research in Psychology, 14*(2), 146–170.

Index

action 21–22, 25, 27–28, 35, 53–55, 77–78; right action 37, 40–41
actors 44–46, 55
affordances *see* moral affordances
agency *see* human agency; participational agency
aims 41, 99
Alzheimer patients 1
ancestral personhood 57, 59
APA style manual 90
argument 79; democratic populism and 108–110
Aristotle 3, 11, 13
articulation 76–78
assumptions 77, 100, 116–119
audience 45, 87, 91–92
authorship 45, 87, 89
availability 87, 91–92

Bakhtin, Mikhail 105, 109
Bazerman, C. 90–91
Bellah, Robert 3
Berlin, Isaiah 61–63, 64–65
Bernstein, R. J. 39
better, the 79–80
Billig, Michael 45, 90
Bishop, R. C. *see* Richardson, F. C.
Bourne, Randolph 107
Brill, S. 99, 102
Brinkmann, S. 13, 40
Brownson, Orestes 107
bureaucracy 3, 86, 103, 112n4

capitalism 107
Chen, Y. 107
choice 27–29, 42–46, 86–91
coercion 42, 88–89, 92

coherence 52
collaboration 45–46, 86–90, 94, 119
Collins, Harry 38
commensurability 52, 62–64
competition 93, 98, 103
conscience 1, 112n1
constructivism 52, 58, 65
context 11–14, 15n5, 97, 117–119, 121–124; culture and 58–59, 63–65; participational agency and 28–30, 32–33; politics and 86–87, 89–90, 94–95; psychotherapy and 73, 76, 78–80; scientific justification and 41–42
credit 42, 45, 86–89
critical thinking 100
culture 6–8, 13–15, 43–44, 51–52, 73–74, 102–105; as context 63; and human nature 52–56
Cushman, Philip 104

Danziger, K. 43
Deneen, Patrick 98, 101–103
deontology 10, 52–54, 73–75
Deresiewicz, William 100
Descartes, R. 106
determinism 9, 21, 28, 111
Dewey, John 4
disclosure 119; world disclosure 31–34
dissemination 43, 45–46, 91, 93–95
Dreyfus, H. L. 12
dualism 3–4, 22, 52, 63, 97; dualist forms of morality 4–12; nondualist forms of morality 12–15

editorial process 87, 92–93
Edwards, Jonathan 107
Emerson, Ralph Waldo 107

emphases 116–119; hermeneutic 24–25, 30–31
empiricism 8–9, 38, 44, 81, 86
entrepreneurial selves 99–101
epistemology 31, 37–38, 43–45, 80, 109
ethics 1–4, 10–11; culture and 52–56, 61, 64; psychotherapy and 74, 77, 81–83
evaluation 61, 81–82; strong 15n6, 24, 75–76, 105

Feyerabend, P. 38, 48n2
forms of life 12–13
Foucault, M. 100
Fraser, Nancy 98–99, 103
freedom 24, 53, 101, 106, 112n2
free will *see* agency
Fromm, Erich 112n2
futurity 27, 29–30

Gadamer, Hans-Georg 4, 32, 39, 97, 118
Garcia-Joslin, J. *see* Richardson, F. C.
Gergen, K. J. 6–7

happiness 1, 7–8, 10, 112n1
Haraway, Donna 39
Harding, Sandra 39
Hatab, L. J. 34
Hedges, Chris 2
Heidegger, Martin 3, 26–27, 30–31, 34, 118
hermeneutic moral realism (HMR) 3, 14–15, 49; Berlin and 63; culture and 51, 53–56, 58–60, 65; inquiry and 116–119; and justification as moral practice 37, 40–41, 48; and participational agency 21, 30, 33–34; and politics 104, 109, 122; pluralism and 61; and psychotherapy 80; and publishing practices 86, 88, 95; Shweder and 63; Taylor and 80, 82
hermeneutics 62, 97, 123; hermeneutic ontology 104–106; and nondualist forms of morality 12–15; and participational agency 22–29, 31–32; and psychotherapy 72–73, 83n3; and scientific justification 38–39, 43, 47; *see also* hermeneutic moral realism
Hesse, M. 40
historicity 27–28

Hmong 55–62, 65
Holiday, Anthony 15n1
human agency 15, 21, 28–29, 90, 102, 118; in the moral space of practice 24–27; and world disclosure 31–34
human nature 27, 52–56, 102

idealism 62–63
identity 1, 14, 72, 82, 100, 103–105, 109
individualism 1–3, 5–8; bureaucratic 112n4; liberal 102–103, 106, 112n3
inquiry 116, 126–127; and interpretive frame 116–119; process of 119–126
institutions 41–43, 45–48, 87–92, 103–104
interpretation 11, 95, 118–119, 121; and culture 56, 59–60, 64; and psychotherapy 72–73, 75–76, 80; and scientific justification 37, 42–43, 45

judgment 95n2; moral judgment 5, 8, 12–14, 21, 54, 90; practical judgment 53; value judgment 121–122
justification 8, 51, 80; *see also* scientific justification

Kant, Immanuel 10–12, 53–54, 97
Kitcher, Phillip 38, 44
knowledge: knowledge practices 48, 87; participational agency and 27–28; politics and 91–94, 109; psychotherapy and 76–77; scientific justification and 41–42, 44–46
Kohlberg, L. 10, 97
Kuhn, T. S. 38

Lambek, Michael 53–56
Lasch, C. 104, 106–112, 112n5
Latour, Bruno 38
Lears, Jackson 100–101
liberalism 101–102, 106
Lilla, Mark 101
limits 97, 101–102, 104–107; a new wisdom of 110–112
Lippman, Walter 109
Loevinger, Jane 95n2
Longino, Helen 38–39, 44

MacIntyre, Alasdair 3–4
marriage 57–58, 72–73, 82–83; marital therapy 76–80

Martin, J.: and A. McLellan 99–100
McLellan, A. *see under* Martin, J.
McWilliams, Susan 106, 112n5
metaphysics 27, 29, 83n3
moral, the 1–2, 4–13, 15n1, 39; and
   culture 62, 64, 65n1; and inquiry
   120–121, 125; moral configurations
   117–119, 123–124, 126; moral
   orientation 14, 24, 72–73; moral
   pluralism 73–74; moral practice
   40–41, 48, 52, 63, 65, 86; moral
   space 21–27, 31, 33, 117, 122;
   and participational agency 28–29,
   35; and politics 97–98, 100–102,
   105–107, 111; and psychotherapy
   71, 75–79, 81, 83, 83n4; *see also*
   hermeneutic moral realism; moral
   affordances; moral ecologies; moral
   realism; *see also under* judgment
moral affordances 37, 41, 48n1; of
   publishing practices 86–95; of social
   science work 42–47
moral ecologies 14–15, 72, 86;
   participational agency and 21,
   24–29, 31, 35
moral realism 4, 8, 11, 31, 116; and
   culture 52, 62, 65n1; and politics
   97–98, 105–106; and psychotherapy
   79, 83n4; *see also* hermeneutic moral
   realism (HMR)
Murdoch, Iris 4

Nagel, Thomas 4, 15n2
neoliberal condition
neoliberalism 100–103, 111; neoliberal
   condition 98–99
nondualism *see under* dualism
normativity 3, 14, 15n4, 40, 57, 76;
   situational normativity 41

objectivism 8–12, 15; and culture 51,
   58–59; and politics 97, 109; and
   scientific justification 38–40, 45;
   see also empiricism; rationalism
objectivity 2, 7–8, 10, 12
ontology 12, 90, 117; and culture 51,
   55, 58, 61, 63–64; hermeneutic
   104–106, 109; ontological turn
   56, 65n1; and participational
   agency 23–24, 26, 33–35; *see also*
   deontology

optimism 102, 107, 110
orientation 23, 92; moral orientation 14,
   24, 72–73, 117; value orientations
   38–40

participation 22, 28–29, 72, 118,
   122–124; *see also* participational
   agency
participational agency 25, 27, 30–34,
   119–120
phenomenology 26
Piaget, J. 10
pluralism 61–63, 73–74
Polanyi, Michael 38
politics 38–39, 43; and democratic
   populism 103–104, 108–110,
   112; and entrepreneurial selves
   99–101; and the failures of liberalism
   101–102; and hermeneutic ontology
   104–106; and the ideal of progress
   106–107; and moral realism
   97–98; and the neoliberal condition
   98–99; and the revolt of the elites
   107–108; and a wisdom of limits
   110–112
polygyny 57
Popper, K. 38, 48n2
populism: authoritarian 98, 107;
   democratic 103–104, 108–110, 112
positivism 51
postmodernism 1–9, 11, 51, 101,
   105–106
practices 12; culture and 52–57,
   61–65; of dwelling 43; inquiry and
   116, 119–127; interpretive frame
   and 116–119; as moral orientation
   72–73; moral pluralism of 73–74;
   moral practices 40–41, 48, 52, 63,
   65, 86; the moral space of 21–27;
   objectivist 45; participational
   agency and 28–35; the practice
   turn 13–14, 97; psychotherapy
   and 72, 75–80, 82–84; scientific
   justification and 46–47; scientific
   practice 40–42, 86; *see also*
   marriage; publishing
progress 89, 99, 103, 106–107, 110
psychology 52–53, 90, 94–95,
   97–100, 111, 117; hermeneutic
   morality in 13; and dualist forms of
   morality 4–12; moral affordances in

42–48; and moral realism 3–4; and
   nondualist forms of morality 12–15
psychotherapy 15, 71, 76–83
publishing 15, 72, 86–87, 95;
   collaboration and credit in 87–89;
   and dissemination 93–95; and the
   editorial process 92–93; forms
   and venues of 91–92; style and
   representation in 89–91

Quine 15n4

rationalism 8, 10–13, 53–56, 61–63,
   86, 97
realism 7, 12, 39, 64, 102; and
   participational agency 24, 32; and
   psychotherapy 72, 75; *see also*
   hermeneutic moral realism (HMR);
   moral realism
relationships 1–2, 42–46, 48n1, 88, 124
relativism 1, 6, 15, 15n1, 38; culture
   and 53, 56, 62–64; inquiry and 106;
   politics and 97; psychotherapy and
   74–75
reporting 90–91, 94–95
representation: in publishing 86, 89–91
representationalism 31
Rescher, Nicholas 54–55, 61–65
research 4, 41–47; *see also* inquiry;
   publishing
revision 92–93
Richardson, F. C. 103, 105
ritual 57–58
Robinson, Daniel 3
Rogers, Carl 6
Rose, N. 99–100
Rorty, Richard 7–8
Royce, Josiah 107

Schwandt, T. 80
Schwartz, Barry 2, 7
Schweigert, W. A. 4
science 2, 4, 34, 74, 89–92, 94, 104;
   see also scientific justification; social
   science
scientific justification 37, 47–48, 86;
   and the failure of objectivism 38–39;
   moral affordances and 42–47; as
   moral practice 40–41; and the value-
   laden nature of science 37–40
Searle, John 4, 13

selfhood 99–100
Seligman, Martin
semantics 15n1, 95
Sewall, G. 104
Shapin, Steven 38
Sheese, Kate 95n2
Shweder, Richard 4, 54, 61, 63–65
Skinner, B. F. 8–9
Slife, Brent D.: and Stephen C. Yancher
   53, 55, 97, 109
Smith, Christian 1–2, 8
Smith, Nicholas 80, 83n3
social science 42–47, 109
Sorel, Georges 107
Stewart, M. 99, 102
Stoller, Matt 104
style 42–43, 45, 86, 89–91
subjectivism 5–8, 75, 97, 109; *see also*
   individualism; postmodernism
subjectivity 2, 5–8, 10–12, 22, 76,
   123
submission 87, 92–93
Sugarman, Jacob 98–100
Sullivan, Andrew 103–104

Taylor, Charles 3, 13, 15, 63, 83n1; and
   the human constant 83n3; and marital
   therapy 76–82; and participational
   agency 23–24, 26; and politics 97,
   104–105; psychotherapy and 71–72,
   82–83; his understanding of morality
   72–76, 83n4
temporality 27–31, 118, 124
time scale 44
Tocqueville, A. de 102
tradition 10–11, 31, 88, 102,
   107; culture and 51–52, 57;
   psychotherapy and 73, 75; scientific
   justification and 37–38, 43–44
transcendence 51, 112
truck driving 13–14, 72

unconcealment 118
use 93–95

value 1–4, 6, 8, 10, 12–15; culture
   and 53, 55–56, 61–64; inquiry
   and 117, 125–126; participational
   agency and 21–24, 26–31,
   33–35; politics and 99, 104–106,
   110; psychotherapy and 71–72;

publishing practices and 87,
90; scientific justification and
41, 43–44, 47–48; and Taylor's
understanding of morality 72–76;
therapy practice and 76–83; value
judgment 121–122; value-laden
nature of science 37–38; value
orientations 38–40; *see also under*
science
venue 86, 91–92

well-being 7, 43, 88, 100
wisdom 101, 107, 110–112
Wittgenstein, Ludwig 3, 13, 15n1
world disclosure *see under* disclosure
Wurmser, L. 111–112
Wylie, Alison 39

Yanchar, Stephen C. *see under* Slife,
   Brent D.
Yeats, W. B. 98

Printed in the United States
by Baker & Taylor Publisher Services